Grail

in the Vales of Avalon

Chris Trwoga

This first edition published in Great Britain in 2001 by:

Speaking Tree Publications

5 High Street
Glastonbury
Somerset BA6 9DP

01458 831800
info@speakingtree.co.uk
www.speakingtree.co.uk

Illustrations and maps © Keith Whittock 2001

Map 'The walks in relation to the Glastonbury Zodiac' produced by Julian Gower.

Illustration of knight on p.49, and all illuminated capitals from Robert Burns' 1939 private publication 'Scots Ballads'

Design/typesetting by Wes Freeman & Bruce Garrard

Reprographics by Bookcraft of Midsomer Norton

Printed and bound in UK by The Bath Press

ISBN 0-9536745-1-7

Grail Quest

in the Vales of Avalon

Chris Trwoga

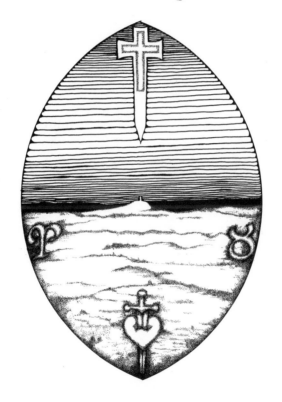

5 High Street, Glastonbury,
Somerset BA6 9DP, UK.
+44 (0)1458 831800
info@speakingtree.co.uk

Grail Quest in the Vales of Avalon

Contents

Grail Quest in the Vales of Avalon

INTRODUCTION

HERE never was such a thing!', many will be tempted to say. But they would be misled by their ill-temper, for the Gral was the very fruit of bliss, a cornucopia of the sweets of this world and such that it scarcely fell short of what they tell us of the Heavenly Kingdom." [1]

Since time beyond remembering pilgrims and poets have set the story of Arthur and the Grail in Glastonbury's unique landscape. In 1191, this association of the heart was launched into history by the 'discovery' of the remains of Arthur and his Queen in an ancient cemetery in the grounds of Glastonbury Abbey. It is Glastonbury's good fortune that, despite many rival claims, the town and its environs have developed the strongest claim to being the very heart of Arthur's Realm.

This book is an invitation to make two journeys. The first is a physical journey through the sacred vales of Avalon in which so many dramas — both real and imaginary — have been enacted. The second is a spiritual journey, where, by travelling the winding paths of the Quest Knight, you might cleanse the spirit of all that ails you.

We will visit those places that the Grail literature of a thousand years has woven into the tales of the Quest, walking on ground hallowed by the feet of pilgrims and — if legend be true — the warhorse of the Quest Knight. In so doing let us hope that we, along with Perceval and Galahad, will experience the presence of that which we call the Grail.

Whatever your beliefs in this matter, I believe that the Quest is a journey of the spirit, and the accomplishment of the Grail a vision of the Eternal, rather than the mere possession of a physical object. It is the same Quest that Jesus accomplished on the Cross, Muhammad in Cave Hira and the Buddha when He attained enlightenment under the Bodhi tree:

7

"In the Queste, the progressive stages of illumination are symbolized by the revelation of the Grail as a movement from what is perceived by the eyes to what is absorbed by the spirit." [2]

The book sets out eight walks. Each is a celebration of Avalon's unique landscape and each connected with some dimension of the myth of Arthur and the Grail. For Maltwood fans, most of her Zodiac symbols will be encountered at some stage, although they do not form the basis of the walks. Seven of the walks set out to explore the countryside of the Grail — the Vales of Avalon. Seven is a significant number in Grail legend. The Grail Knight has to accomplish seven great deeds before he is worthy to enter the Grail Castle. It reflects the seven islands that Arthur must visit in his search for the magic Cauldron of Rebirth in Taliesin's 'Spoils of Annwn', one of the earliest sources for the Celtic origins of the Grail legend. It also, coincidentally, celebrates the seven holy islands that form the Avalonian landscape, each of which bore a chapel and a religious community in medieval times. The eighth walk is called the 'A Meditation on Arthur' and is a celebration of the heart of Avalon — the glorious ruins of Glastonbury Abbey.

The structure of this book is provided by the Grail Story itself, distilled from the medieval writings of Chretien de Troyes and Wolfram von Eschenbach, from Malory's 'Morte D'Arthur' and the unknown authors of the 'High History of the Holy Grail' and the 'Mabinogion'.

Chretien de Troyes wrote what is generally regarded as the first of the great Grail romances, but died before he could complete what became the definitive source for the Grail Legend. Wolfram von Eschenbach, the undisputed giant of German medieval literature, completed Chretien's tale, creating the most profound and mystical of the Grail romances. I regard these versions as the Grail gospels and the other versions as loosely or substantially developed from them. They will be the main sources used in this book.

You will become familiar with the essence of the Grail Myth as we walk, and if time and opportunity permit, it is suggested that the quests are completed in the order set out in the book. Each chapter is based on a significant episode in Perceval's journey to the Grail Castle and in sequence tell the whole story. If time or opportunity does not permit this, the quests can be read and 'walked in the spirit'.

This way, the reader will have the best chance of understanding the story and getting to the heart of the Grail mystery. My aim is that when you've read the book you will be able to regale your friends with a cracking version of the Grail legend!

Each quest is based solidly on the medieval texts and a fresh reading of the Glastonbury landscape. It may disappoint those who prefer their books wrapped in mystical vision quests with regular opportunities to cleanse auras or balancing chakras. Simplicity reflects the minds of the Quest Knights as they come to us from the long past. They were men who did, rather than thought. Perceval, the hero of so many of the Grail legends could almost be described as a simpleton. It was his innocence of soul that enabled him to attain the Grail.

It is the sincere hope of the author that those who follow the path will find what they are looking for.

The Vales of Avalon

Anyone who looks across Somerset from the summit of the Tor will be struck by the sharp contrast between the shapely hills and the flatness of the Sea Moor, or Levels. If you come to Glastonbury in mid-winter or after a period of heavy rainfall you will see that the Moor is prone to return to what it is — wetland. Glastonbury was once an island joined by a causeway to the Poldens to the west and by a narrow isthmus to dry land to the east, where the Shepton Mallet road now runs. The road from Street was still prone to flooding in recent times. To describe Glastonbury as an isle is to describe what was the case at the time of Arthur. In walking this land try to see with the eye of history and imagine a journey by boat when crossing the sea moor.

The Vales of Avalon are under threat. Plans for a bypass and a hospital on the unspoilt northern side of the Glastonbury hills threaten to bury yet more of Arthur's kingdom with the inevitable development that will follow. We may well be the last generation to walk this sacred land before it disappears under an urban sprawl.

A Practical Note

The walks are not designed to be challenging or tiring. They vary in length between two and a half and five miles. They have been set out to provide straightforward parking, access to refreshments en route and to be achievable in a morning or an afternoon. Longer walks could have been designed but this is meant to be journey of the spirit and the walks should be executed mindfully and with plenty of opportunity for rest and meditation. If you cannot complete a walk, the maps provide enough information to enable you to visit the main locations, and after a short stroll, simply enjoy being in the Grail landscape. For those who can but love Glastonbury from afar, it is hoped that the descriptions will be sufficient for the reader to complete the Quest in the spirit.

Paths across the moor can be muddy in winter and even under water in times of flood. The going on higher ground can be just as muddy in wet weather. Walking boots or wellies are recommended in winter and spring or after wet weather, along with a stout staff or walking stick for that Merlin look. British weather is unpredictable, so even on sunny days take a waterproof and light refreshments to boost energy levels. Please leave no litter of any kind — even cigarette butts — and do nothing that may create a fire hazard.

The moor is kept relatively free of water by rhynes (pronounced *reens*) or drainage ditches that carry the water to rivers or 'drains'. Straying from the path on the Moor usually means that your route will soon be obstructed by a rhyne. The designated paths invariably provide the necessary footbridges and stiles to avoid obstructions. Dogs must always be on a lead. Be particularly vigilant with shutting gates as straying cattle can do a great deal of damage. This part of Somerset is working farm country and is not 'open access'. Keeping to the Rights of Way is the best way to avoid long diversions and upsetting the local farmers, whose livelihoods depend on this fragile environment. Whatever your beliefs about land ownership and 'the right to roam' it is the local farmer who maintains the countryside, with its hedgerows and woodland, and it is in everyone's interest to love them for the fantastic work they do in preserving an essentially medieval landscape.

The woodland you will walk through is actively managed and trees are regularly felled. This is necessary to provide for the health of the trees and to facilitate the growth of woodland flora and fauna. The paths and trails through the woods provide the best way to enjoy them and avoid the risk of damaging plants or disturbing wildlife. Remember the old motto — 'take nothing but photographs, leaving nothing behind but memories'.

Love and respect this beautiful countryside.

The Tumulus, Dundon Fort.

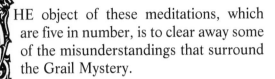

Part 1
Meditations on the Grail

THE object of these meditations, which are five in number, is to clear away some of the misunderstandings that surround the Grail Mystery.

Meditation 1 — Why do it?

Some say the Grail is lost. Others say it is merely the stuff of legend and never was. Lost it may be, but only through a lack of faith. Legend it may be, but it is a legend that goes to the heart of our innermost and deepest felt needs.

To attain the Grail is to achieve a marriage of the flesh and the spirit. It is to look on the face of the Divine just as Adam and Eve did in the Garden of Eden. It is to experience the Eternal in the here and now.

The words are not adequate. The Grail is beyond words.

We should not ask if the Grail exists or does not exist. We should ask if we experience it authentically or inauthentically.

So what?

The pace of modern life, the expression of success in the accumulation of consumer trash, our alienation from Nature, our obsession with the media, our search for truth in the pseudo-spirituality of so many new age religions all take us further and further away from what we authentically are.

The Grail Quest goes inwards and as with the Quest Knights of old you will succeed when you have stopped trying to be what you are not.

Meditation 2 — What is the Grail?

 "With the ambiguity of a metaphor the Grail is many things." [3]

Have you discussed the Grail with others? It has one name, they say, but many forms. Silver cauldron to the Celts, cup, platter, Philosopher's Stone, cruets of sweat and blood caught from the wounds of Jesus — the Christ Child himself brought to the shores of Albion by Joseph of Arimathea. The Chalice of the Last Supper, sought after by Monty Python and Harrison Ford, has homes in the south of France, Bavaria and the Castle of a Scottish laird — not to mention Glastonbury. The Grail has been spirited away by the Templar Knights of crusading fame, the Cathar heretics of medieval France (just before they were massacred on the Pope's orders) and 'discovered' by Wellesley Tudor Pole in a well or sluice not far from the Glastonbury sewage works. The Grail, like God, wears a thousand masks.

In time, the Grail will define itself. You will, if you are worthy, behold the Grail in faith and in truth. To attempt to say what it is before time is to make a false idol of it:

> "Its *symbol* is the Cup, or Chalice, and men have been prone, in their ignorance and folly, to idolise the actual vessal which was never more than the symbol of a deep truth living at the heart of the Faith..." [4]

It may help you to visualise the Grail, just as the Hindu visualises the ineffable Brahman. He will worship a simple stone at the roadside as a manifestation of the Divine. You too will say, "I have seen the Grail!" and your friends will be astonished by the light in your eyes. But do not attempt to describe what you have seen for then you too will create an idol in the minds of others.

Understand that those in modern times who have claimed that the Grail is some existing artifact — usually a cup or chalice — are misguided. Even in the high Middle Ages when tales of Arthur and the Grail Quest were at their pinnacle of popularity, no church claimed to possess the Grail. Pieces of the True Cross, the Shroud, the Crown of Thorns, the Holy Nails, the flesh and bones of countless saints — but never the Grail. Joseph is not described as *bringing* the Grail to Glastonbury because it is not something that could be brought. The Grail cannot be contained or possessed. The medieval mind understood this. The symbol of the cup was seen as a mirror to the soul in which truth dwelt.

> "There is no reason to be concerned with the Grail as a physical object. It is simply not possible to know what it "stands for" precisely. Its success as an image in fact depends upon its being multivalent, open on all sides to the power of evocation." [5]

The origins of the Grail are lost in prehistory. The Celts knew of it long before Taleisin gave us his tantalising glimpses of the Myth in his poem 'Preiddeu Annwn'. The archetypes that become the Grail are probably as old as man himself. In Celtic myth, it is a wonder-working vessel, capable of providing whatever a man might desire, or a cauldron with the power to bring the dead to life. In Chretien de Troyes' 'Perceval', a lance and sword with mystic powers accompany the Grail. In Wolfram von Eschenbach's 'Parzival', it has become a large stone or emerald that fell from the crown of Lucifer and has the power to transmute base things to precious. During the medieval period the 'San Greal', (Holy Grail) became the 'Sang Real', (True Blood), and it is the Blood of Jesus that becomes the Grail, and the Cup of the Last Supper its bearer. All are symbols of a mystery that cannot be put into words.

In his introduction to the 1953 edition of 'A Glastonbury Romance', Cowper Powys said that he believed the Grail older than any symbolism that might be used to define it. No one religious tradition can claim or contain the Grail. It is older than religion itself. In essence, it is eternal and unchanged – as old as the stars themselves:

> "The Grail has its counterpart in the mythology of Greece and in the oldest legends of Wales and Ireland. There are intimate correspondences between it and the traditions that reach us from both the extreme East and the extreme West. It changes its shape. It changes its contents. It changes its aura. It changes its atmosphere. But its essential nature remains unchanged; and even that nature is only the nature of a symbol. It refers us to things beyond itself and to things beyond words." [6]

It is important to understand that it is impossible to know in advance in what form, if any, the Grail will manifest itself to you. The Vision of the Grail is an inner vision, a realization of a greater truth, which may have, as its catalyst, a physical object. It will come when you are ready. It will come when your experiences have made you both worthy and receptive.

This is well expressed by Cowper Powys, who has the Grail appear to his hero in the form of a fish.

"When the vision appeared, and it came sailing into the midst of this bleeding darkness that was Sam's consciousness, healing everything, changing everything, each detail of what he saw with a clearness that branded it forever upon his brain. He saw a globular chalice that had two circular handles. The substance it was made of was clear as crystal; and within it was dark water streaked with blood, and within the water was a shining fish.

Sam's first thought was: "This is the Grail! This is the Grail! It has come back to Glastonbury!" His second thought was: "I must tell Father and Nell about this" His third thought was more realistic.... He thought in his heart: "What is that fish? It is a Tench. Surely it is a Tench!".... To see Christ in the form of a Tench seemed at that moment perfectly natural." [7]

Some say Modern Man has a new Grail. Science, the new religion, is slowly uncoiling God's mysteries under the microscope and will one day fulfill all our desires. They say Science will restore the Garden of Eden and we will once more walk with God.

There is no wisdom in the test tube. They will not see the Breath and the Soul, even though they have counted every last bead of the double helix. Life is infinitely more than the sum of its parts.

But we no longer live in an age of myths! Science is all! Arthur is dead! The Grail belongs to a lost age of castles and kings, of knights and quests — it belongs in the land of faerie! Ask yourself these questions. What remains of scientific truth? What remains of the truth of history? There is a lightness to History, for the past will not return, and if we don't open the history book in the first place it touches us not at all. The schoolboy may well question the relevance of the deeds of the long dead to his daily life. As for Science, no 'truth' lasts for long enough to set it down and by some mystery, the experiment always seems to yield the result we expect. Truth exists in the light behind your eyes and — all too briefly — in what men may agree. Myth illumines that space within. Myth is the bearer of truth

from the Time before Words when naked experience illuminated our world and Ideas and Concepts did not stand in place of what is real. The Grail is such a myth:

> "Myths, therefore, portray a collective image; they tell us about things that are true for all people." [8]

For the modern mind, drowning in a sea of words, the evocative power of the symbol is all but lost. For the medieval mind, the symbol bore a reality more profound than the lost fact of History or the transience of Science. If we do not strive to find what we have lost, our very humanity is at stake.

The modern mind tries to turn myth into history. Is not the *fact* of the Glastonbury Zodiac there on the ground for everyone to see? To subject myth to the scrutiny of the archaeologist's trowel is to misunderstand the nature of myth. To shift myth into history is to tell lies. Worse still, it breeds fundamentalism. The truth of Arthur and the Grail is not dependent on the Arthur of history. The Arthur of history is dead and rotten. The real Arthur sleeps beneath the iron hills. I present the *historical* Arthur merely for your entertainment.

Likewise, the Grail cannot be found by the Long Search. In no physical sense is it *out there*. The role of the Quest Knight is to prepare himself. When he is ready, it will come.

Make no mistake, the Grail is a slippery customer, and the Quest could never be easy. You will be called foolish. There will be failure and setbacks. Hope alone will bind you to the Quest and faith will reward you with tantalising glimpses along the way.

Meditation 3 — The Hero of the Quest

 You want to go on? Then it is time to introduce you to the Hero of the Quest. Stand in front of a mirror — no, do it — and look at yourself. Take a good, long look. The Grail Quest will restore your sight and you will behold your true self for the first time. Do not be afraid. You are made in God's image and the Grail cannot be seen until the vanities of this world have fallen away. You will learn a little about yourself at each step along the way.

It is only by knowing yourself that you may hope to find the Grail.

John Matthews, a Grail Scholar of many years has this to say:

"This surely is the reason for the quest — the desire to penetrate the Grail of one's own being. If the answer lies in some private inner mystery, the reason for the quest becomes a need to identify the inner being with the desired goal." [9]

To know yourself is the prime object of the Grail Quest. Attainment of the Grail comes when we pass the boundary that divides us from the Self and the Self from the Grail. Sadly, we spend so much of our time re-inventing ourselves to suit the popular whim that what we actually are is lost to us completely. Perceval, the chief hero of the medieval Grail legends, fails to attain the Grail when he first stumbles across it because he is too busy observing the proprieties of knighthood (what he *thinks* he should be) to ask the most human of questions about what he has seen.

You too must undo what you have made and shed the mask. For the mask you wear is the same one that hides the face of God.

Meditation 4 — Glastonbury

 "The way is narrow. So let us tread now, through the middle, to the Castle of the Grail and its stone of wisdom, here on earth, which is called the Perfection of Paradise." *Wolfram von Eschenbach*

Where to begin?

Look beneath the modernity that lies like a thin scum on the pool of history. Be still, smell the air on a summer's day, look toward that green hill that filled the vision of the quest knights of long ago. See with their eyes.

Why this hill? Why Glastonbury? Here, of all places, the past and all its magic pours into the present. Having washed over the bones of Arthur's sleeping knights, the Red and White Springs emerge from beneath the Tor, bearing both the legend and the promise of the Grail. Herein lies the entrance to the land of faerie, the Gates of Annwn and no place on earth can lay greater claim to being the Land of Arthur. It was in this earth that the Saxon kings and the Celtic High Kings before them had their bones laid to rest. Crusaders who breathed their last beneath the blood-soaked walls of Jerusalem asked only that their hearts be buried in the shadow of the great Abbey at Glastonbury.

Some say that the sacred land that surrounds Glastonbury is itself the Grail. Carved out of the landscape in ancient times, long before the arrival of Christianity, this land of hills and sea moor was made 'heaven on earth'. In her famous book *Glastonbury, Temple of the Stars*, Katherine Maltwood traced the pattern of the Zodiac and the Grail legend in the Somerset landscape. The Grail was not some cup or other object but the land itself, altered in prehistoric times to match the constellations above. A ten mile radius from Glastonbury had been made, literally, into a "pre-Christian Celestial Temple of the Mysteries":

> "To realise at all the size of the prehistoric 'Round Table of the Grail', one must think in miles not inches, in millennia instead of centuries; for the Temple is ten miles in diameter, it is about 5000 years old, and this counterpart of the heavens corresponds with the constellation figures recognized by astronomers today." [10]

It was this landscape, according to Maltwood, that had inspired the medieval romances of the Grail legends with the correspondences set out in ancient Latin texts. Maltwood was employed to illustrate an English translation of *Perceval le Gallois ou le cont du Graal, (The High History of the Holy Graal)* and became convinced that Avalon was the landscape visualised in the medieval texts:

> "On the last page of the High History we read: 'The Latin from whence this History was drawn into Romance, was taken in the Isle of Avalon, in a holy house of religion that standeth at the head of the Moors Adventurous, there where King Arthur and Queen Guenevere lie,' for the King is one of those giant Cosmic Deities upon which every pilgrim who climbs Glastonbury Tor looks down, but can no longer distinguish." [11]

I cannot support Maltwood's ideas in any literal sense. Many of the features in the land that she incorporated into her Glastonbury Zodiac are the product of modern road making and can hardly be described as ancient. Given the multiplicity of droves, rhynes and field boundaries that cover the Avalonian landscape you can draw almost any shape you wish out of the features you will find on a map or aerial photograph.

But the Glastonbury Zodiac does exist. Like the Grail it exists in the hearts and minds of those who seek it out and find guidance and consolation from it. However fanciful Maltwood's constructions may be, one golden thread of truth remains that binds her to all those who have sought the Grail. She embarked on the Quest in the Vales of Avalon and experienced the Presence of the Grail. The true vision of the Grail may have been denied her but it was in this sacred land that this twentieth century quest knight found her journey's end. She sensed the ineffable truth of the Grail's presence and expressed it by inscribing the heavens themselves on Glastonbury's sacred earth. She, not ancient man, deserves the credit for this wonderful creation, which has inspired three generations, and is a true symbol of a greater truth. When she asks:

> "...Whose was the consummate genius that could see in these rivers and hills a complex circular design, and having envisaged it as a Zodiac, command such skilled labour to carry it out..." [12]

... The answer is Katherine Maltwood!

All attempts to locate the Grail in space and time are doomed to fail. Many other places have been claimed as the land of Arthur and the Grail Quest. Seeking the *fact* of History only serves to cloud the issue. The Grail Castle and the treasure it contains are to be found in the land *behind* your eyes. The Grail will manifest itself to those who are worthy and have sought its grace with a pure heart wherever they may be.

Why then Glastonbury?

In Glastonbury, the dreams and prayers of a hundred generations have sanctified the earth. It is, quite simply, one of Mother Earth's most sacred places and the place where both history and legend bend to sanctify the earth with the deeds of Arthur and the presence of the Grail.

> "But now farewell! I am going a long way
> With these thou seest — if indeed I go
> (For all my mind is clouded with a doubt) —
> To the island valley of Avilion;
> Where falls not hail, or rain, or any snow,
> Nor ever wind blows loudly; but it lies
> Deep meadow'd happy, fair with orchard lawns
> And bowery hollows crown'd with summer sea,
> Where I will heal me of my grievous wound" [13]

Meditation 5 — The Medieval Grail Romances.

Several outstanding authors of the medieval period, culminating in Malory's masterpiece, attempted the theme of the Grail Quest. Scholars are of the opinion that the unfinished 'Perceval' of Chretien de Troyes, written circa 1180, is the earliest major work. There

were undoubtedly older sources, but later authors clearly drew most of their inspiration from Chretien. The tales vary as to which knight attains the Grail and what happens to him thereafter. In Chretien's work it is Perceval who is the one who will attain the Grail. Chretien died before he could complete his masterpiece and it was left to others to finish the tale.

The authors of the Grail stories were dealing with an inherited tradition, which they only partly understood. Around the half-remembered legends of Celtic heroes, wonder-working cauldrons of re-birth, mystic lances that had the power to wreak havoc and swords of power wielded by heroes with superhuman strength they created a new series of legends for a New Age – the age of the feudal knight. Christianity came slowly to the Grail Myth, transforming it gradually into the icons of the age – the chalice of the Last Supper, the Holy Blood, the Lance of Longinus, and the chivalrous knight whose purity of mind, body and purpose was a prerequisite to the attainment of the Grail. Arthur remains incidental to the tale. It is the Round Table that is important, symbolising the shared values of a chivalric age and the impossible heroism and self-sacrifice demanded of its members. Its chief value for those who would seek the Grail lies in understanding the weaknesses of those of its membership who fail in the Quest and the strengths of the one who succeeds.

The fact that we are dealing with the inventions of a medieval author should not be seen as invalidating the potency of the symbol of the Grail. They were expressing a truth as they understood it, re-interpreting ancient verities for a new generation:

"The important thing about Wolfram's Grail is that, though his tale is for amusement and its characters and episodes are frankly fantasies, they are nevertheless understood to be true in a timeless, trans-historic dimension. As in esoteric rites the mystic forms are displayed not in the crude sense of supernatural "facts", but as signs revelatory of insights: so here, the adventures, once of Celtic gods, are presented as paradigms of secular human experiences." [14]

Perceval, the central hero of the earlier Grail legends, is described as the son of a widow and being of royal blood. His father and brothers are dead, killed in pursuing the hazardous lifestyle of the knight. Determined to protect him, his mother brings up her youngest child in ignorance of the ways of the knight, living a rustic existence cut off from the world. Curiously, his mother has not given her child a name – he is the 'Fair Unknown'. His mother also calls him 'Fair Son' and he knows nothing about the rest of his family or his origins.

The tale opens in spring, which is appropriate for a story about new life. One day, whilst hunting, Perceval was approached by knights from Arthur's court. He believed them to be angels and resolved to join their ranks. Ignoring his mother's pleas, who he left lying distraught on the ground, he rides off to seek the court of King Arthur.

On entering the Court, he came so close to the king that he knocked his crown off. Despite this clumsy start Perceval was the only person at the court prepared to tackle the Red Knight who had insulted Arthur and spilt wine over Guenevere. He demanded to be made a knight and because of his noble bearing Arthur is inclined to grant his wish. Armed only with a javelin he succeeds in killing the Red Knight.

Later, he came to the castle of Gurnemanz, who taught him the use of arms and courtly manners, and warned him against talking too much and asking too many questions. The training he received from Gornemanz was to be the foundation of Perceval's success in combat. At the same time, the courtly advice not to ask too many questions will prove Perceval's undoing, when he beholds the Grail for the first time and fails to ask the question Fate demanded of him.

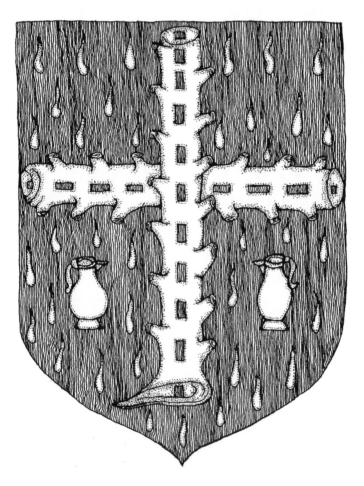

The critical moment came with his meeting with the Fisher King. It is the character of the Fisher King, who has a deep wound in the thigh, which causes him continual great pain, that touches on the most ancient and primordial aspect of the Grail Myth. This is a Winter King, whose wound is phallic and whose potency is thereby lost. With its king impotent the land has become a Waste Land. In a splendid and opulent ceremony, Perceval witnesses a procession in which he sees the Grail. As the Perfect Knight his destiny is to ask the king "What ails thee?"and to ask of the Grail — "Who does it serve?" In so doing the Fisher King would be healed and Perceval would assume his role as the young and vital successor, thus healing the Waste Land. But Perceval fails to ask the question and the moment of redemption is lost. When Perceval awakes the following morning the vision has gone and he is utterly alone.

Years of suffering must follow before Perceval is given the opportunity to enter the Grail Castle once more and attain for himself the Vision of the Eternal.

Let our Quest begin. In so doing, we begin the journey of all thoughtful life — the search for meaning and identity. If we open our eyes a little along the way, we too may attain the necessary wisdom to experience the Grail.

"Among the archetypal images of mankind, the image of a spiritual quest is fundamental, and for this reason is one of the most profound of all the literary themes. It is the 'return' to whatever is nearest to the heart of each man that sets him on his quest. It is the search for the ultimate foundation of his being, for that which lies behind all the images of reality and which creates for him those images. The truth that the quester discovers at the end of the Journey is essentially incommunicable and can be only obliquely suggested. Its multivalency reflects the Woman, the Home, the Patria, the City, the Pot of Gold, the Awakening of the Land cast into sleep, and, ultimately, the deepest secrets of the Self." [15]

1. Wolfram von Eschenbach, Parzival, written circa 1210, trans A.T. Hatto.(Penguin Books, 1986) P.127

2. Frederick W. Locke, The Quest for the Holy Grail, (AMS Press, New York, 1967) P.9

3. ibid.,P.8

4. Frederick Bligh Bond, quoted in The Avalonians by Patrick Benham, (Gothic Image 1993)

5. Frederick W. Locke, P.9

6. John Cowper Powys, preface to 1953 edition of A Glastonbury Romance, (first pub. In UK in 1933 by Macdonald & Co Ltd. This edition Picador 1975) P.XV

7. ibid., P.910

8. Robert A. Johnson, She, (Quoted in H.T. Hansen's foreword to The Mystery of the Grail, Julius Evola, Inner Traditions. Rochester, Vermont 1996)

9. John Matthews, The Grail — Quest for the Eternal, (Thames & Hudson, 1981) P.30

10. K.E.Maltwood, Temple of the Stars, (First pub. 1929. James Clarke & Co. 1982) P.5

11. ibid., P.3

12. ibid., P.116

13. Alfred Lord Tennyson, Idylls of the King.

14. Joseph Campbell, Creative Mythology, Vol.4 of The Masks of God, (Penguin, 1982) P.484

15. Frederick W. Locke, P.3

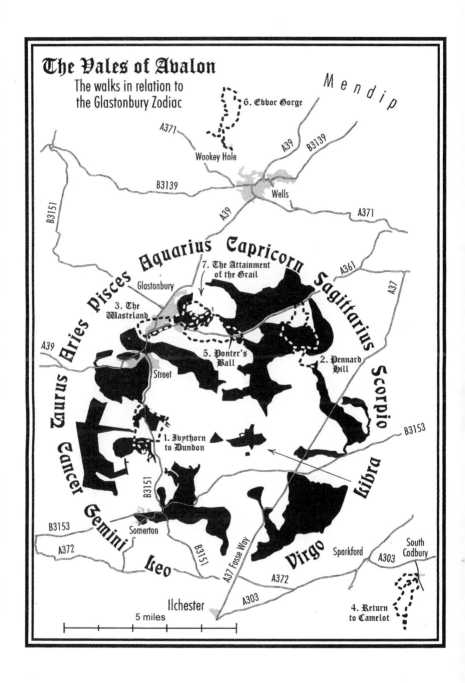

The Vales of Avalon
The walks in relation to the Glastonbury Zodiac

Mendip

6. Ebbor Gorge

A371

Wookey Hole

B3139

A39

B3139

Wells

B3151

A39

A371

Aquarius Capricorn

Pisces 7. The Attainment of the Grail

Aries Glastonbury

Sagittarius

A361

A37

3. The Wasteland

Taurus

A39

5. Ponter's Ball

2. Pennard Hill

Street

Scorpio

Cancer

1. Ivythorn to Dundon

B3153

Libra

B3151

Gemini

Somerton

Leo

B3153

A372

B3151

A37 Fosse Way

Virgo

Sparkford

A303

South Cadbury

Ilchester

A372

A303

4. Return to Camelot

5 miles

27

The First Quest

Ivythorn Hill to Dundon Fort

Perceval and the Loss of Paradise

IVYTHORN and Collard Hill were significant places for Katherine Maltwood. In her 'Temple of the Stars', Ivythorn is the fire sign, Aries, with Ivythorn Hill to Marshall's Elm forming part of the forefoot of the Ram. Here, she believed, Gawain adventured. The country described in the 'High History of the Grail' and referred to by Maltwood is, without doubt, appropriate for the views that can be enjoyed from these hills.

"Messire Gawain rode until he came to a great forest, and seeth a land right fair and rich in a great enclosure of wall, and round the land and the countryside within, the wall stretched right far away. Thitherward he cometh and seeth but one entrance thereinto, and he seeth the fairest land that ever he beheld and the best garnished and the fairest orchards. The country was not more than four leagues Welsh in length and in the midst thereof was a tower on a high rock." [1]

The Grail Legend begins, as does our first walk, in a wood. Chretien de Troyes describes the tragedy that led to Perceval, the son of a king, being brought up as a simple rustic, in fields and woods away from society. Perceval's father was wounded through the thigh and maimed. With the king impotent his land and treasure had fallen to wrack and ruin and he had lapsed into poverty. He had been carried to a manor house in a 'wild forest', where he languished. His two elder sons went off to become knights and to make their fortunes by bearing arms. On their journey home to proudly show their arms and armour to their parents they were both attacked and killed. The older son had his eyes pecked out by ravens and crows and this is how his corpse was brought before his distraught parents. The old king died of grief, leaving his wife alone but for the child in her womb. Thus Perceval, his mother's one remaining comfort, was brought up in a manor house in a forest, utterly ignorant of the ways of chivalry and the courts of kings, ignorant even of his own name and lineage.

Perceval's world was that of a child. His mother sustained his innocence of worldly matters into his fifteenth or sixteenth year to protect her offspring from the fate of his brothers. His life was shaped by a kind of fairy-tale wonderment, where his understanding of himself is based on the myths of the kindergarten. As in all good fairy tales, this fatherless boy will prove to have almost supernatural origins that set him on course for his inevitable, heroic destiny. We too, must return to the forest, to a womb-like innocence and the warm, milky protection of our mother's breast. For all of us, the starting point of the journey is the same. We too, have no past, because our life has just begun.

Let us shed the past, then, and assume the motley garb of the fool. The Quest demands that we begin with no preconceptions, no self-judgement. This is our Age of Innocence. Enjoy it whilst it lasts, for the burden of understanding comes with the Age of Reason.

The walk will take us from Ivythorn Hill south to Dundon and the remains of a hillfort and tumulus. From Dundon we strike east to Compton Dundon and thence north to Hood's monument on Windmill Hill. From Hood's Monument we head west to follow the crest of Collard Hill back to Ivythorn.

The Loss of Paradise

Our walk begins in Ivythorn Wood at the Car Park opposite the Youth Hostel, on the outskirts of Street. To get there by car take the B3151 Somerton Road from Street. The road climbs gently for about half a mile after the last houses of Street toward the wooded ridge of Ivythorn Hill. There is a crossroads at the crest, signposted for the A39 Bridgewater road to the right and Keinton Mandeville to the left. Turn right and park at the car park on the opposite (left hand) side of the road to the Youth Hostel some 300 metres after the junction (A). Better still, check the public transport options available for Street and Somerton. You will want the nearest available bus stop for the Street Youth Hostel.

From the car park, avoid the road and use the footpath in the wood to walk back toward the junction The path runs approximately parallel to the road.

In Maltwood's Zodiac, this stretch of path delineates one of the front hooves of Aries.

Perceval is here because his mother feared that he too would thirst for the glories of knighthood and die bloodily. She hoped to preserve the innocence of her son. She believed that by seeking the quiet places and avoiding the company of fellow humans she could prevent the lust for glory from rising in Perceval's breast. So that he would be ignorant of his noble lineage she did not even give her son a name. When asked his name he always replied that he is called 'dear son', or 'dear master' by those who serve his mother.

Perceval had no identity, not even a name. He represents all those who begin the Quest and go in search of themselves. He represents Man before the Fall, in a kind of guiltless, guileless existence.

Today, you are that child, a foolish innocent, familiar with the ways of woodland and forest, of river and moor and of little else. You recognise the call of each bird and know the difference between the rustle of the wind and the delicate movement of the deer hidden by the undergrowth. This wood is your home and you have known little else since your earliest years. Your world is confined to the visible horizons. The awful fate of your father and brothers is unknown to you.

Your clothes are simple, made by your mother from the tattered remnants of clothes once worn by a king. The motley patchwork of colours and textures is not unlike that of the court fool. It matters little. Your clothes are serviceable and there are none to mock.

Perceval hunted in woods such as these. On a bright summer morning he set out, not knowing that this day would bring the vision that one day would transform him into the foremost knight of his age.

> "It was at that season when trees burst into leaf and grass, woodland and meadow grow green, when in the morning the birds sing sweetly in their own tongue and every living thing is fired with joy, that the son of the widowed lady from the wild, desolate forest got up and found it no effort to saddle his hunter and take up three javelins. Thus equipped he left his mother's house.... So into the forest he goes. The heart within his breast at once thrilled with joy at the fair weather and the glad birdsong he heard, all of which gave him pleasure." [2]

If you choose your time carefully — an early weekend morning before the traffic is about — you will enjoy tranquility and perhaps those early morning mists that can make the sea moors so magical. Otherwise, the drone of passing cars will be a companion on this stretch of path, although the views will more than compensate. The paths through the ivy-covered trees of Ivythorn Wood offer a chance to listen to the same birdsong that lifted Perceval's spirit in the time of Arthur. Walk slowly and think yourself into the spirit of Perceval and the joys of the morning, unmarred by knowledge of the ills of the world.

This is the time before the Fall, when the capacity of man to sin and our knowledge of good and evil is only implicit. Perceval is an innocent, his soul untainted, as indeed it must be to become worthy of the Grail. We all enjoyed this innocence in the mythic state before we ate of the fruit of the Tree of Knowledge of Good and Evil. It is difficult to unthink the pain of the world but we must try. Our cynicism and sense of failure as individuals and as a species, must all be left behind. We need the innocence of a child — even the innocence of an animal that has no real sense of what it is:

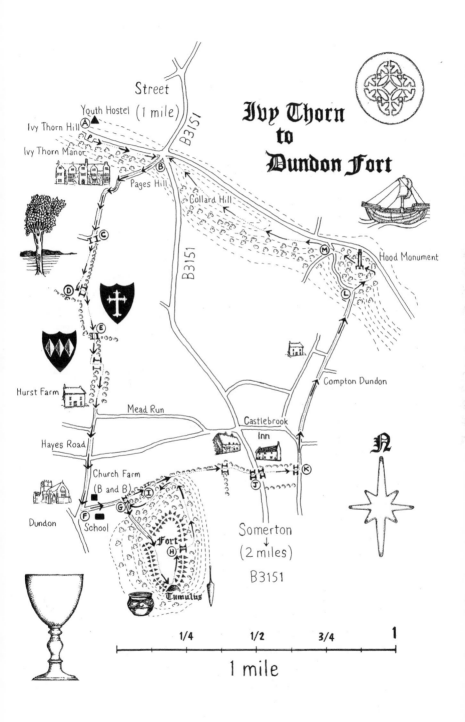

Street

Youth Hostel (1 mile)

Ivy Thorn Hill Ⓐ

Ivy Thorn Manor

B3151

Ⓑ

Pages Hill

Collard Hill

Ⓒ

Ⓜ

B3151

Hood Monument

Ⓓ

Ⓛ

Ⓔ

Hurst Farm

Mead Run

Compton Dundon

Hayes Road

Castlebrook

Inn

Ⓚ

Church Farm
(B and B)

Ⓘ

Ⓙ

Ⓕ

Ⓖ

Somerton

Dundon

School

Fort

Ⓗ

(2 miles)

B3151

Tumulus

Ivy Thorn
to
Dundon Fort

𝕹

1/4   1/2   3/4   1

1 mile

"In Paradise man was not yet man. Or to be more precise, man had not yet been cast out on man's path. Now we are longtime outcasts, flying through the emptiness of time in a straight line. Yet somewhere deep down a thin thread still ties us to that far-off misty Paradise, where Adam leans over a well and, unlike Narcissus, never suspects that the pale yellow blotch appearing in it is he himself." [3]

Just before the junction with the busy B3151 you will come to the narrow road known as Pages Hill. Turn right and follow the road down toward Ivythorn Manor. (B)

As we descend Pages Hill our destination comes into view. Dundon is the wooded, rounded hill in front of us. Dundon village nestles beautifully between Dundon fort and Lollover hill, forming a most distinct shape in the flat sea moor that surrounds it. This once was an island in the marsh, with the fort protecting the Iron Age community from attack. Maltwood identified it as Orion, the giant, or one of the twins of Gemini. She regarded Orion as the oldest and most important of the Nature gods in her 'Temple of the Stars'.

On a hot summer day the trees and high hedges to either side of Pages Hill offer welcome shade and hide until the last moment the view of Ivythorn Manor, nestling in the shade of Ivy Thorn Hill. Here, indeed, Perceval might have spent his youth, magically isolated, as we are now, from the humdrum world. His father had owned such a manor house, and to it Herzeloyde, Perceval's mother, retired with her babe:

"Set on grief, the Lady withdrew from her possessions to a forest in the wilds of Soltane — not to the meadows to be among the flowers. She had no mind for garlands, were they red or of colours less gay, so entire was the sorrow in her heart. To this retreat she took the son of noble Gahmuret for refuge. Her followers had to clear the ground and make it arable." [4]

It is important to think of the world of the Quest as the Grail Masters saw it. For Chretien de Troyes, much was wrong with the world. Beyond the safety of the forest and this small estate lay a wasteland that would not recover until a strong, worthy king came to power. This reflected an ancient belief relating the potency of the king to the fertility of the land. In the time of Arthur, it was literally true that a weak king would inevitably cause the devastation of the land, either from internal dissent or invasion from without.

Continue down the lane past Ivy Thorn Manor. The lane is obstructed by a 'Road Closed' sign and a crude metal and concrete barricade. The barricade is there to stop travellers parking up, and the public footpath continues beyond it. Follow the metalled road until it turns sharp right and becomes a dirt track. (C) Cross the stile immediately ahead of you and follow the hedge line to your left toward Dundon.

You are now on Street Moor and a pleasant stroll follows to Hurst Farm, a kilometre away. The path follows a straight line but a number of stiles are encountered and here and there it switches across plank footbridges from one side of the rhyne to the other.

A noise disturbs the tranquillity of your hunt. A jangling and clanking — strange noises unlike any you have heard before — create a cacophony of crows and rooks and a wheeling and flurry of wings from the trees. You recognise the sound of horse-hooves and voices. There is something not quite human about the sound that puts you on your guard. Then they appear:

"But look! Here come three knights at the gallop as fine as you could wish and armed from heel to crown! The boy thought each a god for sure. Nor did he remain standing any longer but fell on his knees on the path. "Help, God!" he cried at the top of his voice.... When he saw the glittering hauberks and the bright, glittering helmets and the lances and shields, which he had never seen before, and saw the white and the scarlet shining in the sunlight and all the gold, sky-blue and silver, he exclaimed: "Ah, God have mercy on me! These are angels I see here...." [5]

At that moment, a knight rode up to Perceval, giving his horse free rein. He was riding armed in hot pursuit of others who were well away. For a pair of knights had carried a lady off from his country. He was mounted on a fine castilian. His shield was badly battered. 'Who is blocking our way?' he asked and immediately came upon the boy. "Now help me, most helpful God!" was Perceval's earnest cry as he clasped his hands in urgent prayer:

"I am not God," replied the prince, "though I gladly do His will. If you had eyes in your head you would see four knights before you."

"You said 'knights' — What are they? If you lack godlike power, then tell me, who gives knighthood?"

"King Arthur does so. Were you to come under his roof, young sir, you need never blush for the knight he would make of you. I should think you are of noble stock." [6]

For Perceval, innocent and fool, this chance meeting was to transform his life. This is the moment when his spiritual awakening begins. The knights are from another world, leading all the way to Arthur's Court and the Round Table.

To have feet of clay is no bad thing — to be able to draw sustenance from mundane pleasures and our everyday lives. At the same time, we glimpse how things could be. We can conceive of a nobler existence — one perhaps where we devote ourselves to the service of others and the good of future generations, where true love is experienced, and wisdom comes with experience. It is such thoughts that make us restless. If we knew no better we would be content as we are. It is in the nature of being human, however, that we are driven to 'better' ourselves, even if it is only in terms of possessions. Perceval not only desires knighthood — whatever that is — but the trappings of knighthood — and as we shall see, he is ready to kill to get what he wants.

Child-like, he asks the knight about his arms and armour and marvels at their power to protect and destroy. The knight had spoke of Arthur's Court, of the son of Uther Pendragon, whose own kingship was wrapped in tales of magic and wonder. That mystic name rooted itself in Perceval's heart and restless will be his soul until he gazes on the vision of the Table Round and the greatest knights that ever lived.

At the next field boundary climb the stile to your left and cross the plank bridge over the rhyne.(make sure you place your feet firmly on the plank). **(D)** *Follow the hedge line in the same direction for a further 200 metres (the hedge is now on your right) and cross the stile where the field boundary bends left. Look out as you continue to follow the hedge line (now to the left again) for an old iron gate and stile.* **(E)** *Cross over the stile and follow the overgrown farm track that runs by the rhyne. Follow this path until you come to Hurst Farm, with its mix of thatched and tiled roofs.*

At Hurst Farm the road is metalled and is known as Hurst Drove. You walk on in the direction of Dundon, past Mead Run on your left and Middle Drove on your right until you come to Hayes Road. Cross over the road and continue into Dundon until you reach Church Farm guest house. **(F)** *Here we take a sharp switchback left to continue up toward the primary school. Shortly after the school, just past a farm on your right, the metalled road ends. Turn right to follow the track upward to Dundon Fort, first crossing the stile to the left of the five-barred gate.* **(G)**

At the top of the lane you come to a clearing, rimmed by trees and the remains of a wall that formed the main defence of Dundon Fort. *Continuing the line of your ascent cross the clearing to the tumulus known as the beacon.* Records show that the tumulus was dug into in the early part of the nineteenth century. Sadly, as was so often the case, no records of the dig were kept and the notes simply say that human remains were found. There is little doubt that the tumulus is a Bronze Age barrow, which may pre-date the fort by more than a thousand years.

Dundon is an Iron Age hillfort. In England and Wales the remains of 1,350 hillforts survive, pointing to a warlike and heroic age — the true age of the Celts. The South West of England and Wales has the densest distribution of these forts. The visible remains on the ground at Dundon indicate a single defensive rampart, which would have been crowned with a wooden palisade or stone bulwark in its heyday. The occupants of Dundon fort would depend on the already steep sides of the hill to provide the main defence and the commanding views would enable them to see the enemy at a considerable distance. Originally, the rampart would have presented a sheer wall to the enemy. Dundon is defended by a single ditch and rampart and is therefore defined as a 'univallate' fort by archaeologists.

It is impossible to tell if this fort was in use at the time of Arthur, the late fifth century, without further excavation. In those troubled times, with marauding Saxons turning Britain into a waste land, nearby Cadbury Castle was re-fortified. The Celts holding out in the West made use of whatever defence nature and their ancestors provided. Glastonbury Tor was also fortified at this time.

Maltwood described the hill of Dundon as the head of the giant Orion with the earthworks of the fort the sketching out of the ear. There is no historical or archaeological evidence to commend her belief that an ear was deliberately 'drawn' on the hill. In Maltwood's Zodiac, the giant Orion also serves the role of one of the Gemini twins. Mary Caine finds the other twin in the contours of the nearby Bradley Hill. [7]

From the beacon or tumulus, follow the rampart round in an anti-clockwise direction until you face north and toward Glastonbury Tor. Framed by Collard and Windmill Hill and the trees overhead the view of the Tor is quite special.

The distance is important. This is the start of your Quest and you may see the intervening space as your journey to the Court of King Arthur to demand your knighthood. As with life generally, this is your goal for the present — no more. It is the way of things, that having attained one goal, satisfaction is short-lived. Only the Grail is an end in itself.

The tumulus is at the most southern point on the circuit round Dundon's ramparts. If we continue our circuit to the most eastern point, there is a stile over the fence that leads to a path through the wood. (H) Find the stile and follow the path, which spirals gently round the hill to the point where you first began your ascent. It is a well-made path, stepped where necessary, and it is important to keep to it for your comfort. You will emerge, after several minutes just above the stile where you began your ascent (G). Cross the stile and then go through the kissing gate by the five-barred gate to your right. Here you will find a stone-flagged path following the hedge line toward Compton Dundon (I). We will follow this path all the way to the B3151 in a direct easterly direction.

This is pleasant arable land and it is a refreshing change on a warm day when the woods of Dundon can be humid. We are walking toward Copley and Butleigh Woods, and to the North, your next destination on Windmill Hill. Copley Wood forms the body of Leo in the Maltwood Zodiac.

When we arrive at the busy B3151, the path continues on the opposite side of the road where you will see a stile (J). A hundred metres to your left, however, is the Castlebrook Inn and we recommend that the knight takes his ease before continuing with the journey. Take care on your way as there is no pavement and this is a fast road.

This is a worthy place to stop and ponder the ills of the motor car. Compton Dundon is all but cut in two by this busy road. This is an old road linking Somerton, the ancient capital of Wessex, with the great monastery at Glastonbury and the burial ground of the High Kings. This is a road that Alfred the Great would certainly have travelled and probably Arthur too.

Cross the stile (J) on the opposite side of the B3151. The path follows a straight line across the field as a continuation of the path from Dundon fort. Cross over the stile on the far side of the fields and enter Behind Town lane. (K) Turn left and follow the lane up toward

Windmill Hill, bearing right where the lane forks. On the edge of the wood, the road bears sharply to the left (L). At this point you will see a number of paths going off into the wood. Take the path marked 'Reynolds Way', as the path that leads direct to the monument can often be muddy and treacherous. Follow this path through the wood to the crest of Windmill Hill. Here we find the splendid Hood Monument, a commanding pillar to an admiral who fought at the time of Napoleon and became a Knight of the Bath.

A sometimes muddy ascent, sheltered with a fine canopy of trees, leads to this fine column, erected early in the nineteenth century to one of the great admirals of the Napoleonic period, who died serving King and Country in a strange and distant land. The stone ship that is carved atop the pillar is an appropriate motif for those of us who are about to embark on the most significant journey of our lives. Indeed the ship is a frequent motif, even in the earliest of Grail mythology.

In Teliesin's 'Preiddeu Annwn', it is by ship that Arthur goes in search of the Cauldron of Annwn, a magical vessal that has the power to restore men to life, or feed them with their heart's desire. All but seven of Arthur's men lose their lives as they journey to each of the seven sacred islands in search of the magic Cauldron:

> "I am pre-eminent
> Since my song resounded
> In the four-square city
> In the island of the Strong Door.
> The light was dim and mixed with darkness,
> Though bright wine was set before us.
> Three shiploads of Prydwen went with Arthur —
> Save only seven, none returned from Caer Rigor." [8]

And in the latter days of the Grail's golden age, when the Myth had become thoroughly christianised, it is by ship that Galahad, having attained the Grail, sails to the City of Sarras and to Paradise:

> "When they came to the sea, lying close inshore they found the ship which had harboured the Sword of the Strange Belt, and saw the inscription on the hull which said that none should enter unless he firmly believed in Jesus Christ. Standing at the ship's side, and looking into it, they spied the silver table last seen in the

Maimed King's palace. On it stood the Holy Grail, beneath a piece of red samite in the form of a chalice veil. Then, making the sign of the cross, they commended themselves to Our Lord and entered the ship." [9]

The inscriptions on the Hood Monument are instructive, reminding us of the noble qualities of the true knight — the qualities that, one day, Perceval will strive to emulate:

"In the awful scenes of war, in which while they call forth the grandest qualities of human nature, in him likewise gave occasion for the exercise of its most admirable virtues."

We are also reminded of the words of Perceval's mother, when she spoke of the hazards of knighthood:

"But the best of them are fallen, as is commonly seen, with misfortunes overtaking worthy men who conduct themselves with great honour and valour." [10]

Symbolically, we now stand at the root of the horn of Taurus in the Glastonbury Zodiac and we may dwell on what this means for us. Certainly horns and monument are a statement of machismo — and it is machismo rather than any divine calling that has fired the ambition of Perceval.

Perceval was content with his life until he saw the knights of Arthur's court. And so it can be with you or I. We can be happy for a while, finding satisfaction in career, family or the accumulation of material wealth. But happiness is usually short-lived. It only takes the shock of unexpected bad news to shake off our sleepwalking. Bereavement, a job loss, financial difficulties, children leaving home, or a milestone birthday can all bring about the realization of the limited horizon. It takes a glimpse of the sea to realize how shallow were the foundations of our joy. We must venture on a hazardous sea-voyage, risking everything — even our lives — if we are to find what we have lost. What is stirred in us is the undefined yearning for the unknown — that Holy Other, with whom we walked when the world was young and Eden was our garden.

The rustic kingdom of Perceval can be seen as a symbol of that Eden, and he, an Adam before the Fall. Beyond the forests and meadows is a desert, a wasteland. As with Adam, Perceval lost his innocence because of his pride and is forced by the imperative of his experience to leave Paradise and enter the Wasteland. It is a Christ-like journey from his Father's House into the Desert, to encounter the Beast so that he may return to his Father's House once more. [11]

For his mother her worst nightmare was realized and inexorably her heart began to break. Herzeloyde knew that such blood coursed in her son's veins that it would be impossible to change his mind. She resolved therefore, to give him his past and his identity.

"Your father was wounded through the thigh and physically maimed. His great land and rich treasure, which he possessed as a man of worth, all went to rack and ruin, and he lapsed into great poverty. After the death of Utherpendragon, who was king and father of good King Arthur, noble men were impoverished, disinherited and wrongfully brought to destitution. The lands were devastated and the poor people degraded. Your father owned this manor-house here in this wild forest...." [12]

To break free is not easy. Perceval will break his mother's heart and her untimely death will one day come to haunt him. But this is our one chance. We wear the clothes of fools and do not realize it until we compare ourselves with the armour of the knight. The dream of a place at the Round Table may seem foolish and beyond our reach, but the Quest is all and to strive to be free in our hearts is to begin the Quest.

From the Hood Monument a swathe has been cut through the wood in the direction of Glastonbury Tor, providing a magnificent vista of Avalon's sacred hills. This is a good place to take your ease before the walk over Collard Hill and the journey home. It is a symbol, after the all-enclosing wood, of the opening of Perceval's eyes to the wider world and its possibilities. The distant Tor represents the glories of knighthood and the mystery of a journey whose destination is unknown.

Several paths lead from the Hood monument toward Collard Hill. Aim to keep your route parallel with the road and you will descend the last stretch of Behind Town before it joins the main road. Cross Behind Town lane and take the path on the other side of the road leading on to Collard Hill (M). (Do not take the lower stony path as this will take you downward and back to Compton Dundon. Instead, take the path ten metres to the right, where we find a kissing gate set back from the road. Take this path and follow it up on to the crest of Collard Hill.

As we ascend Collard Hill the views to our left and right grow into the most magnificent of panoramas. To the south, King's Sedgmoor stretches flat and mysterious almost as far as the eye can see. In the days of Arthur it would have been under water during the winter months and even in summer great lakes of brackish water, where fish and wildfowl could be hunted, would lie like a string of glittering jewels beneath us. To the north, Glastonbury Tor rises majestically, its lonely tower pointing silently to the heavens. Trees gird the edges of Collard Hill, whereas the crest is kept clear by periodic tree felling. Such clearings would have been created in ancient times to provide grazing for deer. To places such as this, Perceval would come with his three javelins. Ahead, Brent Knoll rises mysteriously from the moor. This too was once crowned with a Celtic hillfort and at sunset is a magical faery fort bathed in red and gold. To the north, the landscape is dominated by the Glastonbury hills, with distant prospects of Wells and the Mendips. Nestling between Wearyall Hill and the Tor is Chalice Hill, where some believe the Cup of the Grail was hid in ancient times.

When you have drunk your fill of the magnificent views head down the gentle slope of the hill toward the two barns at the road junction. At the bottom of the hill cross the stile which will take you on to the B3151. (B) Take great care as driver visibility in all directions is limited. Cross the B3151 and stroll 30 metres or so down Pages Hill and take the path through the wood back to your starting point at the car park.

Perceval left the safety of the wood and the safety of anonymity. He is chasing a dream, a new identity. He faces a future that is defined by vague hopes and half-forgotten dreams. So it is with all our lives. We try to define our future, to plan, to make things happen. But the future is unknown and none can predict how they will feel or what they will become when the Grail is attained.

> "The goals we pursue are always veiled. A girl who longs for marriage longs for something she knows nothing about. The boy who hankers for fame has no idea what fame is. The thing that gives our every move its meaning is always totally unknown to us." [13]

So Perceval rode off in pursuit of an unknown destiny. Was he 'chosen' in some way, a sort of Christ figure? Who knows? Is he compelled by fate or the stars to pursue an inevitable course? Maybe there are just too many accidents and random events in our lives to put things down to a guiding star. Let us choose, rather, to be open to all the possibilities of the future.

1. K.E.Maltwood, quoting from Branch 6, Title 1 of The High History of the Holy Grail, in Glastonbury's Temple of the Stars, (first published 1929, this ed. James Clarke & Co, Cambridge, 1982) Chap. VIII

2. Chretien de Troyes, Perceval. Arthurian Romances, Trans. D.D.R.Owen, (Everyman. 1993) P.375

3. Milan Kundera, The Unbearable Lightness of Being, (Faber & Faber, 1990) P.296

4. Wolfram von Eschenbach, Parzival, written circa 1210, trans A.T. Hatto.(Penguin Books, 1986) P.70

5. Chretien de Troyes, P.375

6. Wolfram von Eschenbach, P.73

7. Mary Caine, The Glastonbury Zodiac, (privately published, Kingston, Surrey, 1978) P.63

8. Taliesin, The Spoils of Annwn, trans John Matthews (Sources of the Grail, edit. John Matthews, Floris Books 1997) P.31

9. Author unknown, Le Queste del Saint Graal, Trans P.M. Matarasso, (Penguin Classics 1969), P.279

10. Chretien de Troyes, P.379

11. Frederick W. Locke, The Quest for the Holy Grail, (AMS Press, New York, 1967) P.66

12. Perceval. Chretien de Troyes v432ff P.380)

13. Milan Kundera, P.122

The Second Quest

Pennard Hill

The Masks of Manhood

PENNARD Hill is one of the least appreciated gems of the Vales of Avalon. A hundred thousand people may camp in its shadow during the Glastonbury Festival of Performing Arts but few will know its name or care about its mysteries. Lying some two miles east of Glastonbury Tor, it is a thinly populated hill, with a small number of farms built on its lower slopes and a gently rolling summit that is almost devoid of settlement. The narrow lanes, bridleways and paths that cross the hill have no destination but the farms and are invariably quiet. This, of all the walks, offers an opportunity for solitude. There are no rat-runs for the motor car here — the steep slopes and narrow, pot-holed lanes offer poor driving conditions but delightful walking.

In Maltwood's Zodiac, Pennard Hill forms the body of the Fire Sign, Sagittarius. Maltwood depicts Sagittarius as a stumbling horse with a helmeted, muscular Arthur springing from his mount.

It is fitting that we should visit Arthur today because it is to his castle at Carlisle that Perceval rode, in the expectation that Arthur would make him a knight. His experience of the knights in dazzling armour riding through the forest of his childhood awoke in Perceval a desire that he inherited from his mother's milk. Writ upon the emerald that is the Gral of Wolfram is the name 'Perceval'. In Perceval's veins flows the blood of the Grail Kings.

When Perceval left his mother, he was a nameless boy, unschooled in everything but the ways of the woodsman. He knew that his mother was a queen but remained ignorant of his father and brothers and their deaths in combat — he was a boy without a history. He sought Arthur to demand knighthood — or rather the glister of knighthood. For Perceval a knight was a demi-god in armour. The code of chivalry was utterly unknown to him.

This reflects our own condition. Stripped of traditional roles, stripped of history and softened by a relatively secure centrally heated environment where the professional soldier fights on our behalf, the male grows ever softer and more feminine. The male psyche, the animus of Jungian psychology, rebels, and drunkenness, drug-taking, street-fighting, reckless driving and one night stands are the pathetic displays of machismo that are mistaken for manliness. Popular culture and the mass media create the myth of what it is to be a man. Somewhere between the feminist myth of Modern Man and yob culture, a boy must find his identity. 'Who am I?' is a problem not only for the individual, but also for the collective male psyche. In a world where money and the multi-national determine our lives and our identities, it has become crucial that we too, feel the pulse of the Sacred Blood within. To be ready to die for a worthy cause is to be truly alive. That men have such feelings is the stamp of an Heroic Age.

The difference for Perceval is that, as a creation of the medieval mind, he moved in a world where the roles of the male as peasant, cleric, knight, and lord were defined and understood. The medieval period was an age when individuality was discouraged. Knights were men of action, not of thought. The demands of chivalry were absolute and the knight knew what was expected of him.

Knowledge of his role as the foremost knight of his age came slowly to Perceval. He began by assuming the role of a knight as a child might play with a wooden sword and cardboard shield.

Today we will trace his first blundering steps along the road to enlightenment and the attainment of the Grail. Arthur will make him a knight and Perceval believed that glory would shine from that alone.

It is the same mistake that a young man makes when he wraps himself in designer clothes and an expensive car and believes that the outside glister reflects a glory within. It is a mask, no more, and the pathetic, naked creature it hides is no more a man for all that.

The walk takes us from 'The Apple Tree' inn on the Shepton Mallet road across arable fields and along country lanes to the crest of Pennard Hill. We then walk along Worthy Lane to Forge Well and follow green lanes and paths to Bradley Brook on the opposite side of the hill. We will have an opportunity to visit Parbrook and the tail of Scorpio. We return by way of Washing Stones Gully and Sticklinch. In wet conditions or for those who find country paths hard going, this walk can be done substantially on tarmacked lanes.

The Masks of Manhood — Pennard Hill

Perceval rode through the forest to find Arthur's Court. In Wolfram's tale, the court of Arthur is at Carlisle, reflecting the fact that the king needs must travel to make his justice felt throughout the land.

The start of our walk is about three miles east of Glastonbury, along the A361 Shepton Mallet Road. Shortly after West Pennard and Piltown villages is a garage on the left incongruously advertising antiques and used cars for sale. Shortly thereafter, in the shadow of Pennard Hill, is 'The Apple Tree', a fine inn offering excellent food. Three hundred metres before the 'Apple Tree' is a lay-by (A) leading to warehouse buildings and you should park here if you are driving and don't intend to use the hostelry. Alternatively, a short taxi or cycle ride along the A361 will bring you to the 'Apple Tree' (B) in a quarter of an hour. A regular bus service runs along the A361 to Shepton Mallet and updated information can be obtained from the Tourist Information Office in Glastonbury. No excuses, it is easy to get to!

In winter and after periods of heavy rain some of the ancient farm tracks on Pennard Hill are boggy and rutted, requiring wellies or walking boots and gaiters. If you are walking in wet conditions a stout walking stick is also recommended to test the depth of the muddy pools and to steady your trek around them. Should it all prove too much the map provides enough information to use the quiet lanes as pleasant alternative routes. But see this as an adventure and enjoy the challenges — the rewards will be all the greater!

On the opposite side of the road to 'The Apple Tree', you should have no problem spotting the 'Public Footpath' sign. Cross the busy A361 with care. The footpath to Willow Farm, which nestles at the foot of Pennard Hill some three hundred metres ahead of you, follows the hedge line to your left.

The first stile you come to **(C)** sits astride what looks like a dramatic earthwork and is in fact the remains of a dismantled railway. Katherine Maltwood refers to the view from the railway station at Pennard and describes how it defined the shape of Sagittarius:

> "Looking up from West Pennard Station, a conspicuous 'linch' can be seen on the hind leg of the horse. Stickleball Lane outlines the whole of the front of this right hind leg from Steanbow up to Forge Well." [1]

West Pennard Station is no more, but we may assume that some of her spirit lingers still at this spot, which she must have visited on her travels.

As you cross the stile look right for a magical view of the Tor, guarding the Gates of Annwn to the West. Behind us, Launcherley Hill, with its steep wooded slopes, obscures the view of the Mendips beyond. From where we stand fine arable fields, planted with corn in summer and deep ploughed during the winter months, slope gently upward to Pennard Hill.

For us, this gap in the great earth bank shall serve as the entrance to Arthur's Castle. Here Perceval encountered a knight armoured in red. Even his sword, lance and shield are entirely enameled in red. The Red Knight proclaimed that he has demanded King Arthur yield up the lands that are his by right. He had taken the wine goblet from in front of the king as a challenge and to assert his title. In so doing, he explained to Perceval, he had spilt wine on Guinevere's lap. This had been clumsiness rather than an intended insult. He asked Perceval to convey to the Queen that he splashed her unintentionally. Further, he would wait outside the gates to joust with any of Arthur's knights who are prepared to answer his challenge.

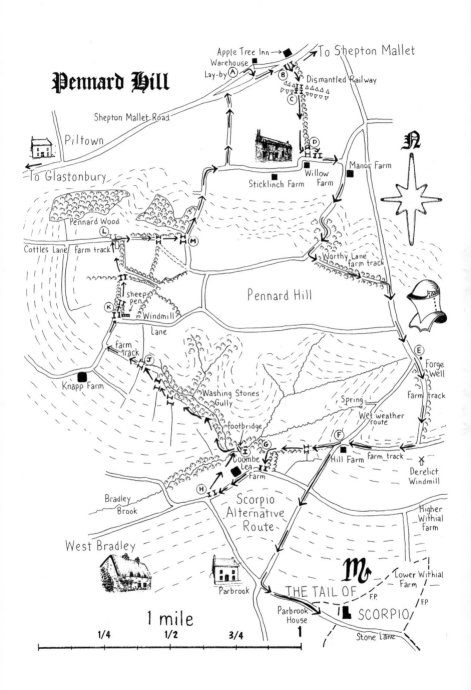

Pennard Hill

To Shepton Mallet

Apple Tree Inn →
Warehouse
Lay-by (A)
(B)
Dismantled Railway
(C)

Shepton Mallet Road

Piltown

To Glastonbury

Sticklinch Farm
Willow Farm
(D)
Manor Farm

N

Pennard Wood
(L)
(M)
Cottles Lane farm track

Worthy Lane
farm track

Pennard Hill

sheep pen
(K)
Windmill
Lane

(E)
Forge Well
farm track

farm track
(J)

Knapp Farm

Washing Stones Gully

Spring
Wet weather route

footbridge
(I)
(G)
(F)
Hill Farm
farm track

Coombe Lea Farm

Derelict Windmill

(H)

Bradley Brook

Scorpio Alternative Route

Higher Withial Farm

West Bradley

Parbrook

♏

THE TAIL OF
F.P.
Lower Withial Farm
F.P.

Parbrook House

SCORPIO

Stone Lane

1 mile

1/4   1/2   3/4   1

Perceval undertook to convey this message to the king with some misgivings. It seemed strange that the king should have received such an insult and left it unanswered. He admired the armour and trappings of the Red Knight with deep envy. He hoped Arthur would be able to equip him in finery to match, once he was made a knight.

*Just before the top of the field as we approach Willow Farm is a stile to the left and a plank bridge across a stream **(D)**. The bridge, not surprisingly, is an old railway sleeper, another reminder of the grotesque decision to abandon railways for roads and increase the isolation of the many rural communities this railway once served. Cross the stile and the bridge and walk to the five-barred metal gate leading to the road. Climb the stile to the left of the gate and turn left to follow the road. At the road junction, turn right to walk past Manor Farm and follow the narrow lane upward to Pennard Hill. Manor Farm is a fine old stone-built house, idyllically facing an apple orchard, with trees colonized by mistletoe.*

Arthur's court was in disarray, with the Knights of the Round Table too fearful to respond to the Red Knight's challenge. Maltwood's image of a king on a stumbling horse is appropriate. So preoccupied was the king that he did not notice the strange young man, dressed in the crude clothes of the Welsh, ride into the hall on his nag.

Perceval was totally unfamiliar with court etiquette, and riding up to the king, accidentally jostled him with his horse. He delivered the message of the Red Knight. But for his good looks, which astonished the court, he might have got rough treatment for his presumption. Without further ado, Perceval demanded that Arthur make him a knight:

"It seems a year to me all this time that I go unknighted. I cannot say it makes me very happy. Now don't put me off any longer but do what it takes to make a knight of me." [2]

A preoccupied Arthur advised the boy to wait until the morrow. Perceval replied that what Arthur is not able to provide him with, he will, with the King's permission, take. He demanded the right to strip the Red Knight of his armour.

Arthur counseled against such folly:

"The man this armour sits on is so formidable that I dare not give it to you. Even now, and through no fault of mine, I am denied his favour and lead a wretched life of it. He is Ither of Gaheviez and has shattered all my happiness." [3]

Insolent Sir Kay, who cared not a fig for the boy, goaded Arthur into accepting Perceval's offer. Perceval needed no further encouragement and raced off to deal with the Red Knight, with the more curious members of Arthur's entourage in hot pursuit.

We follow Perceval and the scatter of squires and pages as they run and ride pell-mell along this ancient lane. As the lane rises, fine old trees provide a welcome canopy in summer. This is a country lane as it should be — rarely visited by anything other than farm traffic and with the silence broken only by the cawing of crows and the wind in the trees. The lane has a moderate gradient, providing plenty of exercise and working up a good sweat on a summer's day. But don't forget to pause when the odd gate offers a distant prospect of the Isles of Avalon — there are fine views to be had as we get closer to the crest of the hill. The lane becomes sunken toward the top and the sound of a stream can be heard mysteriously beneath our feet, all adding to the magic of this place.

At the brow of the hill, there is a public footpath signposted to our right and a narrow lane to the left, known as Worthy Lane. Turn left into Worthy Lane.

In the Maltwood Sagittarius, Worthy Lane outlines a section of the under-part of the body from the stifle joint in the horse's leg. The name 'Worthy' will be familiar to all those who have attended the world-famous Glastonbury Festival of the Performing Arts, which takes place in the Worthy Farm fields below this lane. At the Summer Solstice, the view below us would be of a sea of tents surrounding the bright silvery shapes of the main stages. All that remains in the winter months is the bare skeleton of the Pyramid Stage, standing starkly and incongruously amidst the grazing cows. Whatever the time of year Worthy Lane is a peaceful place, offering magnificent views, the shade of mature trees and good, level walking underfoot.

Perceval rode out to greet the Red Knight:

"The King has made me a gift. I told him, as you asked me, that you spilt the wine accidentally and were annoyed at having been so clumsy. Not one has relish for a fight. Give me what you are riding on and all your gear as well. I'm to be made a knight in it.

If you begrudge me, I'll take back my greeting. So if you are wise you will give it to me." [4]

Wishing to teach the boy a lesson, the Red Knight reversed his lance and thrust Perceval from his nag, so that he tumbled amongst the flowers of the meadow. He used the butt of the lance to give the boy a good hiding. Perceval did not take the hiding as something his arrogance had earned him. Instead he aimed his hunting javelin at the gap between visor and helmet and threw it, piercing the Red Knight through the eye and brain, killing him stone dead.

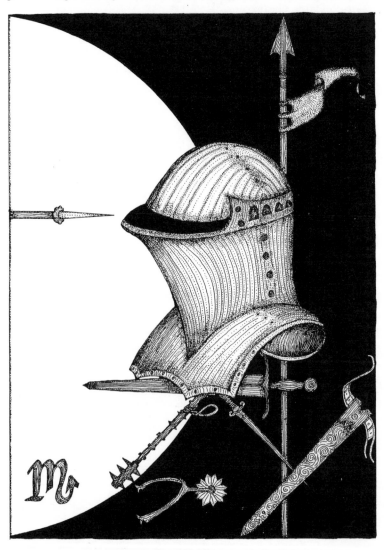

Perceval stripped the corpse of armour and weapons and, with the help of one of Guinevere's pages, donned the armour himself. Once fully armed Perceval demanded his quiver of hunting javelins and received his first lesson in chivalry from the page:

"I will not hand you any javelins:
The Order of Chivalry forbids it."

Perceval has killed a knight with a javelin in cold blood. In other circumstances, this murderous act would have cost him his life, for chivalry forbade the knight the use of missiles such as crossbow bolt, arrow, or javelin. He left the looted corpse of the Red Knight naked in the field, denying an honourable end to a great adversary.

Perceval rode away from the court of King Arthur no wiser than when he arrived. By virtue of the lucky cast of a javelin he killed a man and took both his armour and his identity. It could be described as a David and Goliath story. But it is not, and one day he will weep for his ignoble deed. Chance and covetousness alone has raised Perceval up in the eyes of King Arthur and the Round Table:

"As we have seen, to be a knight was no more to Perceval at first than the realisation of a covetousness; only slowly, through many mistakes, did he develop into what he was intended to be, namely the foremost knight who alone could win the Grail." [5]

Worthy Lane ends at its junction with Stickleball Lane. Turn right and follow the road as it crosses the almost flat fields on the summit of the hill until it takes a sharp turn to the right, immediately after a pair of grey stone cottages at Forge Well (D). Do not follow the road as it turns right but continue straight on, following the green lane that begins just after the cottages. This lane will take us to the southern edge of Pennard Hill and extensive views over south Somerset and Dorset beyond.

The green lane can be boggy and rutted in the winter months or following heavy rain. Check the depth of the puddles if you are in a splashy mood as some can be deep enough to pour in over the top of your wellies. The peace of these lanes makes the hazards of the mud worthwhile. Should you find it all too much or your footwear is not suitable return to Forge Well and use the road to take you down to Hill Farm. Hopefully, it won't be necessary as this ancient green lane offers you a real taste of the Somerset of long ago.

At the terminus of the green lane from Forge Well a 'T' junction offers you a green lane to the left and right. We will be turning right. But before we go we will lean on the five-barred gate awhile and enjoy the distant prospect offered at this point of the walk. On a clear day, you should have no problems making out the flat-topped, tree-ringed summit of Cadbury Camelot in the middle distance. A brisk walk along the 'Monarch's Way' long distance path will get you to Camelot in five hours, crossing the vast image of Virgo that lies stretched out in the plains below Camelot. It is much shorter as the crow flies. Just below us, about a kilometre away, are Lower Withial Farm and College Green. This triangular area of land, bound by two footpaths, forms the sting of Scorpio in the Glastonbury Zodiac. To gaze across to Scorpio is appropriate. The theft of the sword and armour by Perceval will one day bring him much suffering. For the moment, that pain lies in the future — for us and for him — to strike, like the scorpion, when we least expect it. The map provided can be used to visit Scorpio if you plan to visit the entire Zodiac and you are feeling particularly energetic. *Turn right and walk (or paddle!) toward Hill Farm.*

At the end of the lane we come to Hill Farm (F). As the track joins the road we are offered a view of the Tor, peering over the tops of plastic wrapped straw bales. *Walk on to the road that runs round the back of the farm.*

The map now offers an alternative route for those questers who wish to visit Scorpio. This diversion adds a 45-minute stroll to the route along pleasant and little used country lanes. Rights of Way across fields to Parbrook are not recommended, as they have proved unreliable, with crops or electric fences creating serious obstacles. If you do not wish to visit Scorpio ignore the rest of the information given in this paragraph. *Continue on the road past hill farm and down the hill. At the crossroads, a little way down the hill, carry straight on and a seven or eight minute stroll will bring you in to Parbrook. Turn sharp left at the village crossroads and walk on until you reach Parbrook House, the last house on the right.* From the five-barred gate on the left-hand side of the road, an unmarked footpath leads to a grey house. This footpath defines part of Scorpio's sting. Further on, Stone Lane defines the tail. Sadly, one section of footpath that defined the tail has already vanished from the map and these Rights of Way are so little used that they are not visible on the ground. Such is the ephemeral nature of all our creations, including the Glastonbury Zodiac! *To return to Sagittarius, retrace your steps to the centre of Parbrook. At the staggered crossroads continue straight on. At the 'T' junction several minutes down the road from Parbrook, we come to some houses. On the opposite side of the road is a stile. This brings us back to the Sagittarius route at **(H)** on the map.*

*If you do not wish to visit Scorpio, cross the road and then leave it immediately after the farm by going through the gate to the right **(F)**. This track is, in effect, a continuation of the green lane we have just left. Follow the track that runs to the right of the motley collection of farm sheds, where you will usually find stored, somewhat incongruously, a large carnival float. This is one of two floats you should spot on the walk.* Carnival floats on Somerset farmland are a not uncommon sight. There is a century-old tradition of autumn carnivals in Somerset, with the most spectacular taking place in Glastonbury in the first weekend of November. It is a magnificently illuminated evening event, in which local organisations, including many members of the farming community, pit their creative energies to raise money for charity. *Go through the metal gate at the bottom of the field, re-securing the bit of pink string, and continue following the hedge line (now to our left) to the bottom left-hand corner of the field and toward the road. A firmly secured old gate, barbed wire, and briars currently block the actual Right of Way. A brief exploration of the barbed wire fence a little further on at the end of the field will reveal points where you will be able to shimmy underneath with ease **(G)**. Follow the left-hand hedgerow to the gate at the road.*

*Turn right and follow the road to a small hamlet and a road junction about three hundred paces after Combe Lea Farm. On the right-hand side, opposite the junction, is a stile into a field **(H)**. Walk diagonally across the field to its far right hand corner behind Combe Lea Farm and go down the wooded slopes to Bradley Brook **(I)**.*

There are several options for crossing the brook — leap, wade, or balance across the two fallen trees that currently span the stream — but please pause to find a little treasure. If we explore along the brook until directly behind Combe Lea Farm, we find a magnificent footbridge. It offers graceful brick arches, decorated with swathes of ivy, and topped with stone flags. This wonderful footbridge is impossibly narrow and offers no supporting rail. Here is a true Pons

Perilis to test your knightly courage. A fall will land you in the stream some ten feet below so proceed with caution! Here we can replay so many of the tales from the Arthuriad!

Having crossed Pons Perilis and proved yourself worthy of the Quest you will now have to cross it again — it deposits you on the wrong side of Washing Stones Gully. When you have finished playing on the bridge why not explore the gully for a while?

Like us, Perceval was playing at being a knight, with little about him that could be described as 'chivalrous'. Perceval had yet to learn what chivalry meant. Emma Jung, daughter of the famous Carl Jung, summed up what was expected of the true knight in her book 'The Grail Legend':

> "The knight embodies the image of the higher man as it was conceived in that age. For instance, only selected knights might join Arthur's Round Table, those who were masters not only of the knightly arts, such as the handling of arms, riding and hunting, but who also possessed the knightly virtues of fortitude, valour, fearlessness, love of battle, thirst for adventure and above all, constancy and loyalty to the highest degree. In addition...the functions of Arthur's knights were to create order in the land, to prevent wrongdoing and acts of violence, and above all to succour women and maidens in distress." [6]

The opportunity to learn these virtues will come to Perceval purely by chance.

Having claimed the armour of the Red Knight and sent the wine goblet back to Arthur, Perceval rode off into the forest, and travelled for two days and nights without stopping. He and his exhausted horse eventually came to a castle with many towers and turrets. Before the walls of the mighty fortress, a lime tree had spread its branches over the green meadow. In its shade sat a grey-haired man, Gurnemanz de Graharz, the owner of the castle.

Following the advice of his mother, who told him to heed the advice of men with grey locks, Perceval offered his service to Gurnemanz.

Gurnemanz summoned his pages and they led Perceval into the courtyard of the castle. Unsure what to do, Perceval at first refused to dismount from his stolen horse. Finally, overcome with weariness, he allowed himself to be helped from his horse and have his armour removed. His host and servants are aghast at the rough peasant clothes they find beneath the armour. Only the astonishing beauty of Perceval and the transparency of his noble descent prevented ridicule.

Gurnemanz was determined to train this callow youth in the ways of the knight. Having tended to Perceval's cuts and bruises from his encounter with the Red Knight, he persuaded Perceval to part with his simpleton's clothes and don fresh clothes of fine silk brocade trimmed with ermine.

At breakfast, Perceval told the tale of his short life and how he had won his armour. Gurnemanz sighed for the loss of the Red Knight and in the absence of another name, insisted that Perceval should assume his identity and be known henceforth as the 'Red Knight'.

That day Gurnemanz began to teach Perceval the skills of the knight. He learned the use of shield and lance and the art of horsemanship. Perceval stood in place of the three sons that Gurnemanz had lost in battle, and for a while the joy and laughter that once attended his court returned. For a fortnight he entertained Perceval and throughout, the boy grew in his knightly skills and in the manners most proper to the chivalrous code.

During his time with Gurnemanz, Perceval was told to put aside childish things. The excessive bond that his mother had forged must be broken and he must learn to act for himself. For Perceval, the time with the old man is a rite of passage in which he took the first steps on the road to manhood. At the same time, he learned something of what chivalry meant and what it is to be a knight.

One piece of advice proved fateful. Gurnemanz told him to ask few questions and to say little, for therein lay courtly manners. In the court of the Grail King, Perceval's failure to speak will plunge the king and his followers into the darkest despair.

Perceval had grown restless, and expressed his wish to depart. The time had come for Gurnemanz to confer the Order of Knighthood on Perceval:

> "Then the worthy man bent down and fitted on his right spur, it being customary for the man conferring knighthood to fasten on the spur. There were numerous other youths present, and each of them who could attend him lent a hand in his arming.

Next the worthy man took the sword, girt it on him and kissed him, saying he had conferred on him with his sword the highest order created and ordained by God, namely the order of chivalry, which must be free of all baseness." [7]

It was with great sadness that Gurnemanz bade farewell to the young man, who briefly restored the joys of fatherhood to him. Perceval promised to return:

"My lord, I have not yet arrived at years of discretion. But if ever I win fame as a knight such as would entitle me to sue for love, I shall ask you to give me Liaze, the pretty girl your daughter. You have told me of grief past bearing. But if, when the time is ripe, I am able to free you from sorrow, I shall not leave you to bear such a load." [8]

As with so many of Perceval's youthful promises, it was soon forgotten and he never returned to the castle of Gurnemanz. It will be a long time before he is truly worthy of the honour conferred on him that day.

Today, we too become knights of the Quest and begin to take on the burdens that chivalry demands. The Grail Quest is not a road to freedom. To be worthy of the Grail one must first learn how to serve. In self-seeking lies a victory for the Shadow and the disintegration of society. The Light of the Grail will bless all that we do if it is done in a spirit of otherness. It is a road where the grace that comes with self-sacrifice will end the winter darkness and make the flowers to grow. It is the road that leads out of the Waste Land.

The goodness of Gurnemanz put Perceval in mind of his mother, who he had left in a state of considerable distress. As he rode away from Gurnemanz' castle, he vowed to return home and comfort her. He came to the edge of the forest, and, crossing the stream, encouraged his horse up the grassy slopes above Washing Stones Gully.

Washing Stones Gully begins life as a spring high above us, pouring out of the flanks of Sagittarius at the crest of Pennard Hill before carving the deep gully in which the stream flows. Walking in the gully itself to the stream's source is difficult and not recommended unless you have had jungle experience. *Our path runs to the left of the gully and you get to it by scrambling up the slope of the gully and underneath the fence. The path follows the gully to the crest of the hill, to the spring from which this stream flows.*

Katherine Maltwood described this stream as one of the "enchanted springs of Logres"The description of Washing Stones Gully she provides remains accurate to this day and indicates that she once walked this way:

> "On the south side from here fascinating little gorges run down the hill to Bradley Brook. One of them is Washing Stone Gully; mistletoe overhangs it still, and foxes live in the jungle of the undergrowth that spans the streams. Above the calcium carbonate encrusted stones and pools great cultivation linches heave themselves like the ribs of this earth creature." [9]

Perceval is soon distracted by the opportunity of adventure. He chanced upon a fortress, bound by sea on one side and by wasteland on the other. It transpired that the fortress is under attack and those within are suffering greatly from the hardship and privations of a long siege. It is the last bastion of the fair land of Belrepeire. The enemy has seized all the rest.

As we follow Washing Stones Gully up the slope of Pennard Hill, we will encounter three metal five-barred gates. Take care to close all of these gates to prevent cattle straying. By the time we reach the top of the hill, the gully has become a stream in a ditch before finally disappearing at its springhead.

The beautiful Chatelaine of the castle, the fair Blancheflor greeted Perceval. They sat together on a couch, but Perceval, mindful of Gurnemanz' advice not to make idle chatter, remained silent. The damsel waited for some time for Perceval to open the conversation and finally decided to speak first and asked him about his journey. She invited him to dine with her people and to stay the night. After a simple meal — for the siege permitted no better, Perceval retired for the night.

He is not alone for long. Blancheflor entered his chamber and kneeling by his bed, wept until his face is wet with her tears:

> "He was courtly enough to take her at once in his two arms and draw her towards him, saying: "What do you want my fair one? Why have you come here?" — "Ah, noble knight, have pity on me!" [10]

She told Perceval the story of how she has lost all her castles and most of her men-at-arms to King Clamadeu of the Isles. Having rejected his suit for marriage she has been at war ever since. Her land is laid waste. Soon her last castle will fall. Rather than submit to Clamadeu she has a sharp steel dagger prepared which she intends to plunge into her heart. Her tears and story had the desired effect and Perceval offered to fight on her behalf:

"My dear friend, cheer up now tonight! Come up here beside me and wipe the tears from your eyes. Come into this bed beside me, for it's wide enough for both of us. You shall not leave me before tomorrow."She let him kiss her and was not, I think, unhappy to do so!" [11]

The following day Perceval offered to deal with Blancheflor's enemy, in exchange for her love.

He had arrived just in time, for the final assault on the fortress was planned for the morrow, and the enemy was massed in preparation. Perceval rode out that morning and in a fierce battle, fought with lance and sword, defeated Engygeron, the Seneschal of Clamadeu. He spared his life and sent him to surrender to the court of King Arthur. In recognition of his victory, Blancheflor publicly declared Perceval to be her lover and future husband. As luck would have it, two ships laden with provisions came aground on rocks near the castle that day and the merchants on board were persuaded to sell their cargo. With food in plenty, the enemy had no choice but to lift the siege and depart.

With peace and happiness restored to Belrepeire, the nuptuals of Perceval and its Queen took place and that night he lay with his bride. Chretien seems clear about what happened in the marriage bed:

"Meanwhile the one who had thwarted the claim to the land and the maiden, the fair Blancheflor his beloved, takes his pleasure and delight at her side. The land too would have been freely his had he wished...." [12]

Wolfram, who offers us a more naive Perceval, paints a slightly different picture:

" 'Red Knight' though they called him, he inspired little terror: he left the Queen a maiden. Yet she thought she was his wife, and for love of her handsome husband put up her hair in a fillet! Then this virgin bride bestowed her lands and castles on him, for he was the darling of her heart." [13]

Malory's Galahad and the Perceval of the Queste del Saint Graal are worthy of the Grail because they are virgins. They are men of the spirit and the temptations of Eve were resisted. They represent the impact of the Church on this tale and the desire of the clerics to appropriate it to their own ideals, where virginity is the highest state and Original Sin is the dark deed of copulation.

Wolfram allows Perceval to keep his virginity but two days more than Chretien. On the third night following their nuptuals, he discovered, almost by accident, the joys of the marriage bed:

> "He often thought of embracing, as his mother had advised him, and Gurnemanz too had explained to him that that man and woman are all one. They entwined their arms and legs, and if you will allow me to say so, he found what is sweet when near." [14]

A few short days later, having attained manhood by virtue of the training of Gurnemanz and the embraces of his Queen, Perceval departed for new adventures, promising to return to his heart-broken love.

Blancheflor is the foil for the Grail in the Quest legends. Blancheflor was a real woman who awoke in Perceval the conscious and legitimate desires of manhood. It made completeness as a man possible and in true love a finding of the self. Perceval had found a love for a woman that would abide with him always. He attained all the outward trappings of success — and achieved all whilst still in the full flush of youth. In our own age, where youth is adored and fortunes are showered on the talented and beautiful, we may learn from the hollowness of Perceval's achievement at this moment of his history. Chance alone brought him to this pass. He knew this, and responding to the emptiness in his soul, rode back to the forest.

We too must recognize our nature as spiritual and physical beings. The trash of material success, or the arms of a lover, can bring no lasting fulfillment. We are the heroes of our own tale and must expect more of ourselves if we are to find lasting happiness — nothing less than the attainment of the Grail.

Ahead of us, as we go through the third gate, is a green lane leading to the road (J). This little junction is a gathering place for cattle and in wet weather, it becomes a bit of a slurry pit. *Follow the green lane until it joins Windmill Lane.* This stretch of green lane offers magnificent views over Somerset and is particularly fine in early evening when the sun is setting. *At the junction with Windmill Lane turn right and follow the tarmacked road to the brow of the hill. Where the road takes a sharp right (K) go through the metal five-barred gate straight ahead and walk to the left of the farm buildings. Go through a second metal gate a few metres further on to the right and then follow the farm track that runs to the right of the hedge line. At the next metal gate, carry on in the same direction, aiming for a large corrugated iron shed in which farm machinery is stored (L). Just beyond the shed, at the hedge-line, do not go through the gate but turn right and follow the track, which runs by the edge of the hill and a line of fine, mature trees. Go through the gate on the opposite side of the field and continue in the same direction, following the edge of the hill, until you come to a stile by an old metal gate, which provides access to the road (M). Turn left at the road and follow the fine, narrow sunken lane as it descends steeply to Sticklinch. Shortly after Box Farm we come to the road junction with Sawpit Lane. Turn left and follow Sawpit Lane down to the A361. If you used the lay-by to park your vehicle, it will be directly opposite. (If you parked at 'The Apple Tree' it might be more pleasant to bear right instead of left at the junction with Sawpit Lane at Sticklinch and follow the lane back to Willow Farm, taking the path back from Willow Farm to the Apple Tree.)*

Perceval aspired to be a knight but did not understand what it meant. Instead, he assumed a mask —the outward trappings of the Red Knight. Victory in battle and marriage to a queen has raised him up but this shallow glory does not reflect the man behind the mask.

Jung points out that the assumption of such masks is automatic as we grow up. We assume a persona that is suitable for the society of which we are a part. We present ourselves to the world as a member of a clan, race, profession or class and not as an individual with our own identity. The wearing of the mask cannot be separated from the values that we attach to it. The danger of the persona — as with the character of Peer Gynt — is that we choose the wrong persona and thus lose ourselves. The mask should represent characteristics and ideals that are worth striving for. Badly chosen or abused, the mask leads to hypocrisy and worse:

> "The persona deteriorates into a mere mask when it no longer fulfills its purpose but only conceals a void or worse, therefore falsifying the essential nature of the individual. At the same time, the persona-like clothing offers a defence against the world without which the individual would be all too vulnerable. But

when the ideal is wrongly chosen, when it is unattainable or unsuited to the individual nature, then striving towards it can often lead one into error." [15]

We may compare Perceval's condition with that of Peer Gynt, who wanders the world from end to end, assuming one mask after another and getting no closer to the heart of things:

"You're no Emperor. You're just an onion.
Now then, little Peer, I'm going to peel you.
The outermost layer is withered and torn;
That's the shipwrecked man on the upturned keel...
And inside that is the digger of gold;
Its juice is all gone, if it ever had any...
And here is the Prophet, fresh and juicy;
Like the man in the proverb, he stinks of lies.
What a terrible lot of layers there are!
Surely, I'll get down to the heart?
No — there isn't one! Just a series of shells
All the way through, getting smaller and smaller!" [16]

For Peer Gynt, when all the layers of the onion are gone there is nothing left. For us, salvation lies in the discovery of the Grail within.

1. K.E.Maltwood, Glastonbury's Temple of the Stars, (first published1929, this ed. James Clarke & Co, Cambridge, 1982) P.36

2. Wolfram von Eschenbach, Parzival, written circa 1210, trans A.T. Hatto.(Penguin Books, 1986) P.85.

3. ibid., P.86

4. ibid., P.87

5. Emma Jung & Marie-Louise von Franz, The Grail Legend, trans. Andrea Dykes, (Sigo Press, Boston 1986) P.54

6. ibid., P.54-55

7. Chretien de Troyes, Perceval, Arthurian Romances, Trans. D.D.R.Owen, (Everyman. 1993) P. 396

8. Wolfram von Eschenbach, P.99

9. K.E.Maltwood, P.38

10. Chretien de Troyes, P.401

11. ibid., P.402

12. ibid., P.413

13. Wolfram von Eschenbach, P.110

14. ibid., P.110

15. Emma Jung, P.60

16. Henrik Ibsen, Peer Gynt, 1867. trans. M.Meyer. (Methuen 1987) Act V, Scene V

The Third Quest

The Beckery, Bridies Mound, Pomparles Bridge and Wearyall Hill

The Waste Land and the Fisher King

HE grail was of pure refined gold. And this grail was set with many kinds of precious stones, the richest and most costly in sea or earth. Exactly as the lance had done, they passed in front of the couch, going from one room into another. The young man saw them pass, but did not dare ask who was served from the grail, for he kept continually in his heart the words of that wise gentleman." [1]

In Wolfram von Eschenbach's 'Parzival' there are two disabled kings. The old Grail King, enfeebled with age, has retired from the world. All that sustains him is a single wafer from the Grail with which he is fed each day. His successor, the Fisher King, Anfortas, lies wounded through the thighs in the Grail Castle. Together they represent kingship that has grown feeble with age or damaged by impotence. The Fisher King's wound prevents him riding or hunting and leaves him in constant pain. His only pastime is fishing — hence his name — although he continues to live in splendour. Beyond the gates of the Grail Castle, the land is in a sorry state. The King and the Land are one, and so his impotence means the land will no longer bear fruit. He languishes, awaiting a worthy successor who will ask the crucial question and take his place. If none are worthy to wear his crown then all will be lost and death will stalk the land.

The origins of the Fisher King story are lost in prehistory. It is a tale of the land, which each year grows old and weary as autumn turns to winter. The land, like the king, must die and be reborn. In Celtic legend, the king is the husband of the land. He makes it fertile. If the king becomes impotent, as the Fisher King has, the land will become barren. It is the role of the Grail Hero to restore the king. His reward will be the Grail Kingdom and the immortality it promises.

Albert Camus in his book 'The Myth of Sisyphus' gives us a much more down to earth understanding of the pointless suffering of the Fisher King. Camus' hero is the Sisyphus of Greek mythology. Sisyphus, like the Fisher King, is condemned to suffer unendurable torture, in his case, to forever push a huge rock up a hill that will only roll down again when he has pushed it to the top. Sisyphus, when very old, had decided to test his wife's obedience by telling her to cast his corpse into the market place on his death. This she did. Appalled by the apparent lack of reverence and love shown by her actions, Sisyphus obtained permission to return to earth from Pluto in order to chastise his wife. Having returned to the sun and the sea and all the pleasures of life, he resisted all the attempts to recall him to his proper place. Consequently, the gods punished him:

> "Mercury came and seized the impudent man by the collar and, snatching him from his joys, led him forcibly back to the underworld where his rock was ready for him. You have already grasped that Sisyphus is the absurd hero. He is, as much through his passions as through his torture. His scorn of the gods, his hatred of death, and his passion for life won him that unspeakable penalty in which the whole being is exerted towards accomplishing nothing." [2]

Sisyphus is sentenced to endless torment for defying the gods — in essence, for being human and refusing to accept the inevitability of death. Sisyphus knew what he had lost, yearned for the Eden of earthly life, and refused to let go. Likewise, the Fisher King represents the absurdity of human existence, with its inevitable, pointless suffering that can only be relieved by death — or by the love of the one who asks the question:

"What ails you?"

What relevance does the 'Waste Land' have for us?

We live and move in our own spiritual wasteland. We feel impotent to change our lives or the world. This inability to ask the crucial questions leads to our land and lives being laid waste by forces we believe are beyond our control. The Grail represents a kind of Garden of Eden, the myth of a Paradise Lost where there is no death and the earth is forever fruitful. We know what we have lost. We die, yet we can conceive of a world where death is unnecessary. We suffer the injustice and hazards of an indifferent world, yet we can imagine a life where goodness is rewarded, and evil does not thrive.

To understand our common loss, that is, to understand our intuition of what life *could* be is to understand the universal experience of the Fall. The Waste Land is the loss of Eden and our consciousness of the sword of fire that prevents our return. A thousand tales recount how Paradise was lost — from the story of Pandora's Box to the Serpent and the forbidden fruit. Myth or no, the story reflects the human condition, the intuition of having fallen from some better state through our own fault.

The Grail Vision is a glimpse of the Paradise we have lost. To attain the Grail is to return to Eden and make it possible for others to do the same.

In the twenty-first century, the idea of the Waste Land has another meaning. This will become only too apparent as you pass Glastonbury's ugly industrial park, smell the sewage works and ponder the dereliction of the Morlands factory, the ground polluted with the poisonous waste of a hundred years of tanning leather. Attractive and much-needed houses lie empty and crumbling close to the unwholesome atmosphere of Beckery. For twenty-five years, this ruin has affronted the senses of visitors entering Glastonbury from Street. The Regional Development Authority has recently purchased Morlands. Now that it is in public hands there is hope of progress. Pray that Mother Earth will be respected this time, as the planners and local community decide what is to be done with the Morlands site.

How have we reached this pass? Why has Western Civilization — of all the civilizations that have existed — set out to systematically destroy Nature?

The heart of the problem lies in the way we see the world and ourselves. The bible, the conceptual foundation of the West, preaches a *transcendent* God — a God *out there*. It preaches that we are creatures and that our relationship with our Maker is disordered. When we turn in on ourselves, we do not find God, but a sinful, created soul. Thus, God and His creation are separated. God is not seen as *immanent* — within — as He is in Eastern Philosophy. Nature is also disordered, having become, since the Fall, the kingdom of Satan, and therefore has to be bent and twisted and tortured until it conforms once more to the Divine Will. We blame nature — the Earthly Paradise — for causing us to sin in the first place.

Thus, we created a trinity of opposites — the Self, God, the World, fighting against each other and fighting to the death. We, the victors, despise ourselves for what we have done and our sense of loss is overwhelming. God is dead and we live in a world which, by our own hand, is dying too.

We may have abandoned the theology in the twenty-first century but we have not abandoned the lie. We must undo the lie in order to heal our souls. Only then can we heal the land. It is in this spirit that we begin our quest.

Katherine Maltwood saw Wearyall Hill as part of the gigantic Grail zodiac that ancient man traced out of Avalon's landscape. Wearyall Hill was part of the Water Sign Pisces, with a second fish formed out of the high ground on which Street's cemetery lies, to the North of the A39. The choice is appropriate, both because Wearyall Hill is decidedly fish shaped, and there is an ancient association with the Fisher King.

> "From King Fisherman's Castle — which is the Wearyall Hill Fish effigy — one looks down towards the north west on the prehistoric lake villages of Godney and Meare. It was doubtless their idol, for a fish was supposed to swallow the sun as it sank down into the sea, thus explaining King Fisherman's sickness and death." [3]

Wearyall Hill is associated with Joseph of Arimathea. Legend says Joseph rested here with his followers — hence 'weary all' — and planted his famous flowering staff. His story and that of the Fisher King were woven together by the medieval romances, making Joseph the first of the Grail Kings and the one from whom all others are descended. Legend informs us that Joseph brought cruets containing the blood and sweat of Jesus to Avalon — which became symbols of the Grail.

As in the tale of old we must now enter the Waste Land and seek the Castle of the Grail.

The walk will take us through the town's industrial park and then to the River Brue. We will walk along the banks of the Brue to visit the site of the medieval Beckery and Pomparles Bridge before crossing the A39 and ascending Wearyall Hill, returning to the town centre via Hillhead.

The Waste Land

Our walk begins at the square at the bottom of the High Street (A), where the steps of the market cross provide precarious ramps for the towns' youthful skate-boarders. The cross, modelled on the Eleanor crosses of Edward I, is relatively recent, having been replaced in 1846, following the destruction of the original in a drunken frolic. Those in the town late on a Friday evening will realise that little has changed down the centuries.

Turn right into Benedict Street and walk down to St. Benedict's Church. Originally a chapel dedicated to St. Benignus, it was built to align with the great Abbey Church and is first referred to in 1215. It is believed that the church was built to house the bones of Beonna, a local holy man from Meare, who was later mistaken for St. Benignus, disciple and successor to St. Patrick and, according to William of Malmesbury, his immediate successor as Abbot of Glastonbury. The association attracted many Irish pilgrims, with legend and tradition claiming that St. Patrick and, St. Beonna or Benignus had ended their days at Glastonbury.

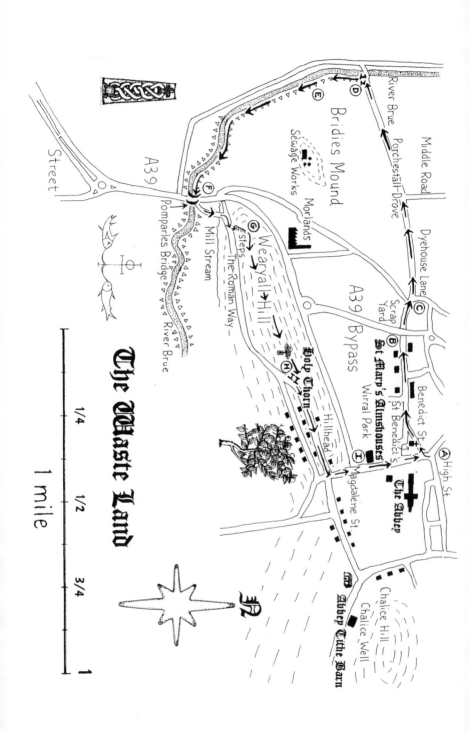

I make this reference now because our walk takes us round the entire area of Beckery, which was once known as 'Little Ireland', because of the number of Irish who settled on the island in ancient times. The Rev. Lionel Smithett Lewis, in his book 'Glastonbury, the Mother of Saints', argues that the name Beckery is derived from Beg Eri, or Little Ireland. Others argue that the derivation is from 'Bee-keeper's Island'. [4]

The Chapel of St. Benignus remained a chapel until 1846, when it became a Parish Church in its own right.

Just beyond, and to the left of the West entrance to St. Benedicts is the 'King Arthur' pub. There are no known historical associations between the building and the hero of our quest but it is an excellent hostelry for a bit of local atmosphere and frequent live music from the local talent.

Continue walking down the street toward Wirral Park.

As we come to the end of the street, with its motley collection of modest late Victorian terraced houses, we arrive at Wirral Park on our left. Here we get our first view of Wearyall Hill, which we will later ascend, with its many-layered associations with Grail myths. Today's park is only a small remnant of the original park. In the thirteenth century, Wirral Park was a 200 acre deer-park, belonging to the abbey. It remained a deer-park until the Dissolution, when the 200 acres became common grazing land. Now it is home to a cricket pitch, tennis courts and housing developments, as well as an industrial estate.

At the end of the road (B) we come to a wall and signs for the Peat Moor Visitor Centre. These signs guide us to a pedestrian crossing. Cross the bypass using the crossing and head for Snow's Timber Yard. We walk across a little roundabout to the right of the timber yard (C) to Porchestall Drove, which we follow until it crosses the River Brue. To our left once stood a large mound, known locally as 'Glastonbury Castle'. It is probable that it was the remains of a motte and bailey castle. Excavations at various times have unearthed everything from Neolithic flints, to Arthurian Age pottery. Iron smelting took place here in medieval times. It is one of the crimes of Glastonbury's modern development that it was levelled in 1972 to make way for the industrial park.

Happily, the ugly industrial development and scrap yard soon gives way to open sea moor. We can reflect on the fact that in Arthurian times the fields around us were marsh and open water. A traveller to Glastonbury would arrive by boat, landing at the foot of Wearyall Hill or the monastic sanctuary of St. Bride's Mound. At drier times of the year it might have been possible to cross by the ancient causeway from Street. To this day the moor is prone to flooding from November to May. It becomes a wasteland, unusable until it has dried sufficiently to allow the return of sheep or cattle grazing in spring.

Porchestall Drove is usually quiet, going as it does to nowhere in particular, and is a good place to get into a meditative mood. Like all the droves, it has rhynes to either side, choked with weeds and algae in summer and dark threatening water in winter. To your right, as you walk toward the Brue, is a fine view of the unbroken ridge of the Mendip Hills with the intervening moor segmented by lines of pollarded trees.

We follow Porchestall Drove until we come to a bridge, which takes the road over the River Brue (D). The distance is little more than a kilometre — too short a distance to do any more than dawdle but distance enough to clear the mind.

It is not necessary to cross the bridge to continue the walk but it is the first of three bridges we will encounter. The three bridges put us in mind of the adventures of Gawain in 'Perlesvaus' or the 'High History of the Holy Grail' when three bridges over three rivers that Gawain must be crossed to reach the Grail Castle.

"...As he approached the castle entrance he saw there were three long and terrible bridges to cross, with three great rivers flowing beneath." [5]

Our bridge is small and squat — an ugly girder construction. The Brue flows lazily beneath it. The only time you might approach with trepidation is in the season of flooding when the swollen river may well have burst its banks and water laps over the bridge.

To your left, just before the bridge, you will find a post marking the public footpath to 'Pons Perilis'. Open the gate (or squeeze through the gap if the string fastenings defeat you) and enter the field. Follow the footpath along the raised bank of the Brue towards the Perilous

Bridge a mile away. The path is pleasant underfoot in dry weather, but cattle can turn sections of it into mire in winter and spring.

The moor in front of you has always been a sacred barrier. The Brue drains what was once a lake. A great stretch of water lies between you and the Isle of Avalon.

On the lake is a boat from which two men fish.

"In the evening Parzival came to a lake. Some fishermen whose lake it was had anchored there. One of those in the boat was wearing clothes of such quality that had he been lord of the whole earth they could not have been finer. His hat was of peacock's feathers and lined inside. Parzival asked the Angler in God's name and of his courtesy to tell him where he might seek shelter for the night, and thus did that Man of Sorrows answer: "Sir, he said, "I know of no habitation beside the lake or inland for thirty miles. Nearby stands a lone castle. I urge you to go there. What other place could you reach before nightfall? If you do find your way there I shall take care of you myself this evening...Take care — some tracks lead to unknown country, you could miss your path on the mountain-side, and I would not wish that to happen to you." [6]

We accept the offer of the Angler, though you do not yet know that he is the Fisher King.

To continue with our walk is to cross a boundary. The Grail and the Castle that guards it is a spiritual place that lies somewhere between heaven and earth. Briefly, the veil that conceals the Grail will be lifted. Do not expect the experience to bring happiness. To see beyond the flaming sword is to experience the pain of separation from all that your heart desires.

As we walk toward Beckery, we can see that this once beautiful place, with its rich history of Irish saints and Arthurian myth, is the most spoilt corner of Avalon.

All is not lost. Raise your eyes beyond the Waste Land and we have a wonderful view of the Tor, and if we turn round to face the way we have come, the unbroken sweep of the Mendips is there to remind us of how insignificant this blot on the landscape really is.

But don't be too distracted. We are looking for a small round-topped stone, a little like a grave marker just below the path, which marks, so the legend reads, where the holy well of Saint Bride once was **(E)**.

The stone is decorated with a cross, carved in Celtic knot-work. The part-buried inscription reads: 'This stone marks the traditional spot of St. Bride's Well.' The actual location of the holy well is lost. The stone was moved to its present setting in the 1920s and is believed to be about a hundred metres from its original location.

It was in this well that a Cup was 'discovered' in 1906 that was hailed in the national papers of the day and by several scholars and mystics as the Grail made manifest in the modern world.

The story made national news and there were those who came to reverence the Cup as the Grail, or the Cup of the Last Supper. On July 26th 1907, the Daily Express carried the headline:

"Mystery of a Relic; Finder believes it to be the Holy Grail; Two Visions; Great Scientist Puzzled; Discovered at Glastonbury.... Dr Goodchild entertains the belief, consequent upon his strange experiences, that it is the cup which the Saviour used at the Last Supper, and which, according to the Glastonbury Legend, was brought to Britain after the Crucifixion." [7]

Wellesley Tudor Pole, who later founded the Chalice Well Trust, had little doubt about the significance of the find:

"For some five years from the present date I have been interested in Glastonbury, its legends, its mythology. My pilgrimages have taken place either on the first weeks of each year or around Bride's Day or both. Almost from the first day that I was there on pilgrimage, I have felt convinced that a great find was about to take place and I have dedicated myself to the search for the 'Holy Grail'... The efforts (of the Allen sisters) resulted in the bringing of the Holy Cup, encrusted with mud to the surface of a certain Holy Well.... As a result of this, my sister was sent down to bring back the Holy Graal to a shrine prepared for It."

Signed — Wellesley Tudor Pole. February 22, 1907. [8]

For some time afterwards a veritable cult grew about the reverencing of the Cup, whilst scholars continued to debate its authenticity. Over time interest in the Cup faded. It is now in the care of the Chalice Well Trust.

The significance of this event does not lie in the authenticity or otherwise of the Cup. The whole is an expression of the spirit of this place and of that undefined yearning that is the motive for the Grail Quest. Countless pilgrims have gazed from where you now stand across the watery wastes and the deep morning mists to the Sanctuary of Avalon and sensed the nearness of that 'Holy Other'. The space that separates us from the Mound of St. Bride represents our separation from the Divine.

A little beyond the Bride's Well stone, a rhyne crosses underneath the path to enter the Brue via a sluice. The spot offers an excellent view of the long, low mound of St. Bride as well as the dereliction of the

Morlands Factory. The view of Bridie's Mound is the best you will get short of seeking the farmer's permission to approach the mound directly. Should you do so there is now nothing to see but scrub and nettles.

Excavations were carried out in 1967-68 sponsored by the Chalice Well Trust. The remains of a monastery dating back to Anglo-Saxon times was uncovered at the heart of which was a small chapel and a tomb that contained the remains of a body that may date back to the sixth century. These bones are in all probability the remains of the hermit or saint whose presence first hallowed the ground for Christ. As well as an array of monastic buildings, the excavation also revealed a cemetery. All but two of the 63 bodies excavated were male, indication that this was a cemetery for the monastic community. [9]

Here stood a timber chapel of great antiquity, replaced in late Anglo-Saxon times with a stone building. The Irish connection and the fame of Glastonbury as a whole ensured that this sacred place, already of great antiquity a thousand years ago, was popular with pilgrims. For us, the significance lies in the fact that this was a sacred place at the time of Arthur.

Before the coming of Christianity — who knows? The link with St Bride, or Bridget who legend says visited the mound in 488 AD, possibly has its roots in the worship of a Celtic female deity. According to John of Glastonbury, writing in the early 1400s, there was an oratory dedicated to St. Mary Magdalene here — another important female figure.

A local organisation — the 'Friends of Bridie's Mound' — are fighting to ensure that this sacred earth is not swept away in any future development of the area. They would like to see the mound cleared, the remains of the chapel consolidated, and the immediate area planted with an orchard. They argue that it could, and should be a place of pilgrimage and quiet reflection once more.

There is also a strong Grail link. At Beckery, according to John of Glastonbury, King Arthur had a vision of Mary as Mistress of the Earth and Queen of Heaven, and her Son, Jesus. It was this vision that led to Arthur becoming a Christian. The story describes how Arthur lay sleeping at the Convent of St. Peter on Wearyall Hill, when he dreamed three times of an angel who commanded him to go to the

Chapel of St. Mary Magdalene at Beckery. The tale is in fact an adaptation from Branch 1 of the 'High History of the Holy Grail'. In the tale Arthur rides to the chapel and there experiences what can only be described as a Grail Vision, although hidden powers deny him entry to the sacred space.

"Thitherward goeth he and alighteth, and it seemeth him that the hermit is apparelled to sing the mass. He reigneth up his horse to the bough of the tree by the side of the chapel and thinketh to enter thereinto, but, had it been to conquer all the kingdoms of the world, thereinto might he not enter. And he looketh at the holy and seeth at his right hand the fairest Child that ever he had seen. On the left side was a Lady so fair that all the beauties of the world might not compare them with her beauty. 'Sir', said she, 'You are my Father and my Son and my Lord, and guardian of me and of all the world. King Arthur looketh at the window behind the altar and seeth a flame clearer than any ray of sun nor moon nor star, and evermore it threw forth a brightness of light such that and all the lights of the world had been together it would not have been the like." [10]

We will walk the remaining few hundred paces to the stile that will take us to the relentless traffic of the A39 and Pons Perilis or Pomparles Bridge (F). Cross the stile. You are now on the Perilous Bridge that must be crossed before the Grail Castle can be entered. *Carefully cross the busy road to admire the view of the Tor from the far side.*

Pons Perilis is no longer beautiful. The present Pons Perilis consists of a stone bridge of twentieth century provenance married to a concrete span, which widens the original bridge. It is hardly a fitting structure given its long history and Arthurian links.

It is hard to visualise — as Leland the Tudor historian describes — 'a Bridge of Stone of four arches communely caullid Pontperlus where men fable that Arture cast his Swerd.' — that from this bridge Sir Bedivere gave up Excalibur to a samite clad hand emerging from the water. Sadly, legend does not offer the place where Arthur lay bleeding as Excalibur was thrown into the marsh, but we may imagine that it was here that Excalibur was last seen by Arthur and the eyes of men. Bright Caliburn, flung high into the darkening sky, as the sun descends beyond the Black Mountains of Caerleon, is grasped by a slender female hand and drawn into the shadowy waters of the mere.

But the traffic is an irritation at your back and if the wind is in the wrong direction, the whiff of the sewage works masks the sweet summer smells of the countryside. To our right, the village of Street encroaches, where tourist hordes engage in 'retail therapy'. Forget all this. Ignore the superficial layer of the present, which is gone even as we contemplate our next step. The legend of the past is embedded in this landscape forever. We will see the lake again in the dawn light, when the mist lies on the moor and the Tor is once more the sacred Isle of Avalon.

This is the end of the story, you say, not the beginning. Surely, the abandonment of the Sword of Hope leaves a land without a king and the Grail Quest at an end.

But we are not in time now but in the world of time past, where all that is history and all that is myth exist together in the space behind our eyes.

He is here! Look for him, for his wounds are deep and soon he will be taken from you. Hurry or you will never know what was lost when the Grail was hidden from men's eyes!

Listen for the King's dying breath upon the wind. He is close now. He calls to you. Kneel beside him. Cradle his head in your lap. Feel the sorrow of his passing. The vision of a healed land is about to die. He is in dreadful pain, for Mordred's death blow has cut through his helmet and shattered his skull. His greatness is done. With fear and sorrow, he faces the closing darkness. He remembers those he has loved and the simple fleshly pleasures that will not come again. He will not see the sun rise or smell the morning air again. The kiss of a lover and the taste of wine on his lips are already a memory.

He remembers the times before the Quest, when all those he had loved were sat about him — the time of the Companionship of the Round Table.

With the King gone, the Waste Land has returned.

We forget what we have lost. Paradise, nothing less, is what is lost, the Garden of Eden, the time before the Fall when Man walked with God. We need not be religious about this. Can we imagine what it would be like to live in a world from which pain is banished? No, it is not that we forget. We live with the pain of our loss constantly. Death — the loss of everything — is imminent for all of us. We know how things should be.

Pomparles is the second bridge that we have encountered. This is in keeping with the story that requires the questing knight to cross three perilous bridges before they can attain the gate to the Grail Castle.

"As Gawain approached the castle entrance he saw that there were three long and terrible bridges to cross, with three great rivers flowing beneath. It seemed to him that the first bridge was about the length of a bowshot but less than a foot wide. It looked narrow indeed, and the river beneath was wide and deep and swift. He did not know what to do, for it seemed to him that no-one could cross it either on foot or on horseback." [11]

An old knight told him there is nothing to fear and beckoned Gawain to cross. Gawain was ashamed that he tarried so long. Had he not just confessed his sins and repented of them? He had nothing to fear but death itself. He took courage and crossed — and the bridge suddenly became as wide as he could wish for.

Ponder for a while and meditate upon the idea that Gawain had nothing to fear except fear itself. When he understood this the obstacles in his path vanish. It is time to ask ourselves of our own fears and how many times we have failed to cross the bridge because of our lack of courage. We live in the shadow of what might have been because of our fear of the narrow bridge. Cross the bridge this time and make yourself a promise that you will cross those future bridges too.

Walk up toward The Roman Way. En route, you will cross over Mill Stream. The stream flows through Beckery and passes by Bridies Mound. It is the third time we have encountered a bridge and its crossing marks our entrance to the Isle of Avalon and the land of the Fisher King.

> "And so Gawain came to the third bridge. Because of what he had now seen he felt no fear, and the third bridge was not like the others: all across it were marble columns, with a pommel on each one, which seemed to be of gold. Then he looked at the gate ahead of him, and there he saw depicted Our Lord on the cross, with his mother on one side and St. John on the other; all in gold they were, with precious stones that blazed like fires." [12]

After a row of stone cottages to your left and a modern stone-clad bungalow with stone horse heads on the gate posts turn left up a flight of stone steps that lead to a stile and Wearyall Hill (G). Once on Wearyall Hill turn right to walk up to the crest of the hill.

Pause. You are now at the gate. The entrance to the Grail Castle marks the boundary dividing the world of the flesh from the world of the spirit. This is an Otherworld, a place that exists nowhere on earth but belongs to the spirit and the imagination of those worthy enough to find it. And in spirit we now enter the Grail Castle. Whatever feasting takes place, whatever glories are presented to those fortunate enough to enter, when morning comes all will have vanished. You will witness the Grail, but witness it without understanding. You will witness the suffering of the Fisher King, you will see how the Grail gives to all their hearts' desire, and yet you will not ask the question.

King Fisherman, Keeper of the Grail, lies on his bed at the heart of the Grail Castle:

"The lord of the castle had himself seated on a sling-bed over against the middle of the fireplace. He and happiness had settled accounts with each other, he was more dead than alive. Parzival with his radiant looks now entered the hall and was well received by him who had sent him there — his host did not keep him standing but bade him approach and be seated.

A company of grave knights was sitting where they were presented with a sad spectacle. A page ran in at the door, bearing a lance from whose keen steel blood issued and then ran down the shaft to his hand and all but reached his sleeve.

At this there was weeping and wailing throughout that spacious hall, the inhabitants of thirty lands could not have wrung such a flood from their eyes. The page carried the lance round the four walls back to the door and then ran out again, whereupon the pain was assuaged that had been prompted by the sorrow those people had been reminded of.

After this came the Princess. Her face shed such refulgence that all imagined it was sunrise. This maiden was seen wearing brocade of Araby. Upon a green achmardi she bore the consummation of heart's desire, its root and blossoming — a thing called 'The Gral', paradisal, transcending all earthly perfection! She whom the Gral suffered to carry itself had the name of Repanse de Schoye.

The faithful Princess then set the Gral before his lordship. The Gral was the very fruit of bliss, a cornucopia of the sweets of this world and such that it scarcely fell short of what they tell us of the Heavenly Kingdom. For whatever liquor a man held out his cup, whatever drink a man could name, be it mulberry wine, wine or ruby, by virtue of the Gral he could see it in his cup. The noble company partook of the Gral's hospitality.

Parzival well observed the magnificence and wonder of it all, yet, true to the dictates of good breeding, he refrained from asking any question."

Alas that he asked no question then!" [13]

Sadly, Perceval believed the correct thing to do was to remain silent. He believed that it was not proper for a knight to speak out of turn and ask unnecessary questions. Perceval was so eager to impress that he denied his own nature and said nothing. Many years must pass before he was to have the chance to ask the question again. His silence condemned him and the best knights of his age to years of wanderings from which many did not return. He condemned the Grail King to further agony and the land to waste away.

Walk to the crest of Wearyall Hill where benches provide rest for the weary or contemplative. The first two benches we encounter face Beckery. From this vantage point, we can truly appreciate the unfortunate positioning of Glastonbury's industrial park and the lack of any attempt to plan or prettify. If only we had asked the question!

Toward the summit of the hill, there are more benches and these, fortunately, face Butleigh Moor and the mystical Tor. From the summit, we can see the ruins of the Abbey and much of the town — it offers indeed, the finest view of all that is Glastonbury. It offers respite from the Waste Land, and the prospect of a healing at a future time.

For symbolic purposes, our separation from the Tor represents our separation from ourselves and from the Grail.

We saw that the Fisher King was wounded and in great pain but we did not ask the question 'What ails thee?'. We didn't ask it because it did not seem proper, within the code of conduct we have been taught, to ask unnecessary and personal questions. At a deeper level, we perhaps don't care enough to ask such questions meaningfully of others and — worse still — to ask the same question meaningfully of ourselves.

"What ails thee?"

If we are able to identify our own wounds as well as the wounds of others, it helps to understand how we got them. Often the deepest wounds are self-inflicted, although we all too often blame others for our pain.

As we begin our descent towards Hill Head we come across a lonely thorn protected by iron railings. This is the location of the original Glastonbury Thorn. According to legend, Joseph of Arimathea planted the staff that became the flowering thorn. This spot was a place of pilgrimage in its own right, even after the Dissolution of the Monasteries. It took the fanaticism of a puritan of Cromwell's time, who cut down the ancient thorn, to end the cult of the Holy Thorn.

The thorns that grow in St. John's Churchyard and the Abbey grounds are descended from the original thorn that grew on this hill. They are of a variety to be found in Palestine, and do indeed flower at Christmas time, giving some credence to the story of the origin of the Holy Thorn.

This lonely thorn is still visited by latter-day pilgrims and often you will find scraps of ribbon tied to it — an ancient Celtic tradition thought to bring good luck and healing. If the mood so takes you why not tie your own scrap of fabric to the tree and pray to your God for luck on the Quest. The cloth should be from something you have worn or used so that there is a connection between you and the thorn. Thus, when you are descended and home part of you will remain in this lonely spot until wind, rain, and the passage of time does to the cloth what it does to all.

We will part from the Quest here, *taking the path down to a stile to the right, which gives access to Hillhead* **(H)**. This is one of the ancient habitations of Glastonbury, high above the floodwaters of bygone years. Once this was a poor part of Glastonbury where tiny, thatched cottages concealed poverty and the wind howled through broken casements on winter nights. Now rather more up-market properties jostle each other to enjoy the view over Butleigh Moor to the south. *To return to the start of the walk follow Hillhead down toward the town.* At the bottom of Hillhead, we touch upon Fisher's Hill, which leads down to Butleigh Moor. *We will turn left and cross the road to Magdalene Street.* On our way back, we pass St. Mary's Almshouses **(I)**. The chapel is well worth a visit in its own right as a place for meditation and reflection. Why not call in and spend a few minutes quiet in the garden or the chapel? This was a custom beloved of questing knights at the end of a day's adventuring.

Sit quietly in this place and ask the question — alas too late!

"What ails thee?"

Perceval is not ready and he is blinded by the conceit of his recent knighthood. It is the paradox of the Grail Quest that he must become innocent again in order to be worthy of the Grail. We too are not ready. We have travelled but a short distance on the road to self-discovery. As with Peer Gynt, we must continue the endless quest in the hope of finding what we have lost.

"Tell me, then! Where was my self, my whole self, my true self?
The self that bore God's stamp upon its brow?" [14]

1. Chretien de Troyes, Perceval, trans. D.D.R.Owen, (Everyman edition, J.M..Dent, 1999) v.3320, p.418

2. Albert Camus. The Myth of Sisyphus, trans. Justin O'Brien, first published 1955. (Penguin Twentieth-Century Classics, 1975) P.108

3. K.E. Maltwood, Glastonbury's Temple of the Stars, first published 1929. (This ed. James Clarke & Co, Cambridge, 1982) P.65

4. Revd. Lionel Smithett Lewis, Vicar of Glastonbury, Glastonbury, the Mother of Saints, (St. Stephen's Press, Bristol, 1925) P.14ff

5. The High Book of the Grail, a translation of the thirteenth-century romance of Perlesvaus, trans. Nigel Bryant. (D.S.Brewer, 1996) P.77

6. Wolfram von Eschenbach, Parzival, written circa 1210, trans A.T. Hatto.(Penguin Books, 1986) P.121

7. Patrick Benham, The Avalonians, (Gothic Image publications, 1993) P.74ff

8. ibid P.59ff

9. Philip Rahtz, Glastonbury, (Batsford/ English Heritage 1993) P.118

10. The High History of the Holy Graal, trans. Sebastian Evans. (James Clarke & Co, Cambridge, undated re-print) P.11

11. The High Book of the Grail, 1996, P.76

12. ibid. P.77

13. Wolfram von Eschenbach, P.123ff

14. Henrik Ibsen, Peer Gynt, 1867. trans. M.Meyer. (Methuen 1987) Act V, Scene X

The Fourth Quest

Return to Camelot

BROTHER, had you known our mighty hall,
Which Merlin built for Arthur long ago!
For all the sacred mount of Camelot,
And all the dim rich city, roof by roof,
Tower after tower, spire beyond spire,
By grove, garden lawn, and rushing brook,
Climbs to the mighty hall that Merlin built." [1]

Cadbury-Camelot is one of the gems of the Somerset countryside. It is a great, flat-topped hill, carved by the Celts into a fortress with precipitous ramparts and a maze of defences. Occupied and fortified from the Stone Age to the beginning of the medieval period the fort has been in use longer than any comparable defensive site in Britain. Until recent times, it was relatively free of trees and its dramatic shape attracted a wealth of local folklore. Faerie folk dwell here, there are magical wells, and within the hollow hill, Arthur sleeps, riding out with his knights at full moon toward the distant Avalon. For those seeking mighty walls, turrets, and towers there will be disappointment — but for a low grass-covered wall ringing the summit no above ground stonework remains. Camelot always was and still is a place of the heart and the imagination.

Situated a few miles north of Sherborne, hard by the pretty village of South Cadbury, Camelot is a half-hour car journey from Glastonbury and no more than an hour and a quarter or so by bicycle along quiet country lanes. For long distance walkers it sits astride the Monarch's Way, a long distance footpath that links Glastonbury to South Cadbury on its journey across Somerset. This is one of two outstanding footpaths serving the area, the other being the Leland Trail. Both are well maintained and signposted and clearly indicated on new OS maps.

What evidence ties Cadbury to the glittering fancies of Malory and Tennyson? The antiquary, John Leland, first published the claims of folklore in 1542.

> "At the very south ende of the chirch of South-Cadbryi standith Camallate, sumtyme a famose toun or castelle, apon a very torre or hille, wunderfully enstrengtheid of nature. Much gold, sylver and coper of the Romaine coynes hath be found ther yn plouing...The people can telle nothing there but that they have heard say that Arture much resortid to Camalat." [2]

The myths of Arthur and the Grail have their origins in the dim and distant past, pre-dating any written history. Camelot, on the other hand, is a medieval invention. There is no reference to it in literature prior to Chretien de Troyes tale and all the medieval references, from Chretien to Malory, leave the location vague. But tradition and folk memory is as good a reason as any for this association of the heart, and in recent years, archaeology has lent a hand in supporting the claims of tradition.

In the 1950s, pottery turned up by the plough on the summit of Cadbury Castle was identified as belonging to the so-called 'Dark Age' Arthurian period, that is, to the late fifth and sixth centuries. [3] Excavations begun in the 1960s revealed a complex site, with settlements from the Neolithic period to the eleventh century, when Ethelred the Unready established a late Anglo-Saxon settlement and coin-mint on the hill. Amongst all this archaeological complexity, an impressive fortification from the time of Arthur was identified. Of the handful of Iron Age hillforts that are known to have been in use at the time of Arthur, Cadbury Camelot is by far the largest. Cadbury is ideally placed to defend the British kingdom of Dumnonia against the Saxon assaults.

Excavations revealed the walls of the Arthurian fort at Cadbury were timber braced and faced with dry-stone walling, re-using stone from the Roman period, and the walkway above the wall was protected by a timber palisade. At the south-west entrance to the fort the foundations of a fine gateway were located, including the original cobbled road surface, as well as evidence of a timber gate and look-out tower.

From the same period the post-holes of a timber feasting hall, some sixty by thirty feet in size, were discovered. The feasting hall would have been where the warrior king fed and feasted his war-band, the hearth companions that legend would transform into the knights of the Table Round. A typical war-band at the time of Arthur might have numbered a hundred men. To combat a major threat war-bands would combine under a 'dux bellorum' or war-leader to a size of perhaps three hundred men. But why re-fortify eighteen acres for so small a force? Cadbury's Arthurian fortifications are much bigger than any other of the period. Leslie Alcock speculates that Camelot's warlord had a much larger garrison to accommodate, combining the forces of several petty kings, and for such an army Cadbury alone was large enough:

"Cadbury was outstanding at this time among British fortresses in terms of the size and strength of its defences.... With every justification we can think of Arthur and his troops feasting and carousing — like the Gododdin army in the hall of Myddynog Mwynfawr — in a hall similar to that at Cadbury; and riding out to battle through a gate-tower like that at the south-west entrance." [4]

Tradition, archaeology, and romance bend, therefore, to make this the spot where the historic Arthur held court, the Round Table was built and the Grail Quest was first announced.

And here indeed Arthur may have spoken the words:

"Gracious lords, you will embark very soon on the Quest for the Holy Grail. And because I know that I shall never again see you all assembled as you are today, I would have in the meadows of Camelot a tournament so splendid that after our death our heirs will talk of it still." [5]

The Round Table

If you are travelling to Camelot by car from Glastonbury, the most straightforward route is to take the B3151 from Street to the turning for the A303 junction a couple of miles before Ilchester. From the junction, turn left for the A303. Follow the A303 until you see the sign for North Cadbury on the left. Immediately after leaving the A303 turn right to cross the bridge over the A303. Approximately a kilometre down the road and two hundred metres after the church of South Cadbury, turn left into the specially provided car park. For the cyclist security bars are provided but please leave no valuables with your cycle. (I usually cycle to Camelot and keep my bicycle with me as there is excellent cycling on these quiet lanes.)

If time, lack of energy or disability does not permit the completion of the full walk then the section of the walk in the fort itself is very rewarding.

From the car park entrance (A) we turn left (away from South Cadbury church) and follow the quiet lane toward Eastcombe Farm. Walking on the road is not ideal but this is a quiet lane, with little to distract, and can only muster the odd car even on a bank holiday. After a short distance, we see a farm gate to the right of the lane. Pause here, rest your elbows on the five-barred gate, and admire the fine view of the impressive ramparts that once protected the court of Arthur. Continue, after this pause at the gate, in the same direction.

Do not turn up Craigs Lane but continue walking down Church Road until you encounter the junction with Stonehill lane, which rises gently toward Parrock Hill.

The beautiful young man, who had so briefly graced the court of Arthur, had won fame far and wide through his heroic deeds. It was Arthur's wish to welcome him to the fellowship of the Round Table. For his part, Perceval had chosen to remain alone, spurning the companionship of Arthur and his knights, whilst sending him tokens of his success. Arthur could contain his patience no longer and decided to find the mysterious knight and bring him back to Camelot to receive the honours he had earned. He ordered his retainers to

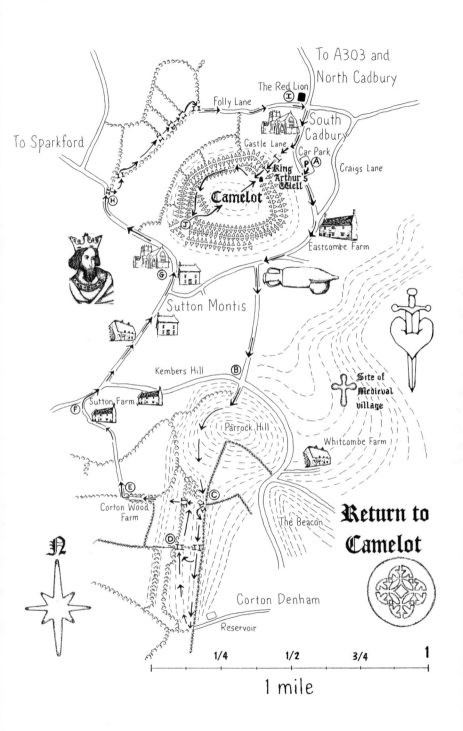

To A303 and
North Cadbury

To Sparkford

The Red Lion
Ⓘ ▪

Folly Lane

South
Cadbury

Castle Lane

Car Park
Ⓟ Ⓐ

Craigs Lane

Ⓗ

King
Arthur's
Well

Camelot

Ⓣ

Eastcombe Farm

Ⓖ

Sutton Montis

Kembers Hill

Ⓑ

Site of
Medieval
village

Ⓕ Sutton Farm

Parrock Hill

Whitcombe Farm

Ⓔ

Corton Wood
Farm

Ⓒ

The Beacon

Ⓓ Ⅱ Ⅱ

Return to
Camelot

Ⓝ

Corton Denham

Reservoir

| 1/4 | 1/2 | 3/4 | 1 |

1 mile

prepare to depart to find the knight. So it was that Arthur and his court left Camelot at Michaelmas, the feast of St. Michael, when the trees are in blossom. Accompanied by his nobles and retainers he searched for eight days and nights for the man who styled himself the Red Knight.

Perceval's mother had once dreamt that her child would become a fierce dragon. As he rides out on the feast of St. Michael, in his suit of blood-red armour, Perceval is more dragon than dragon-slayer. Proud and alone he rides, having stolen both the identity and the life of the Red Knight. He engaged many a knight in combat, killing for no reason other than that the world should know his glory. Michaelmas reminds us of the tale of how St. Michael drove Lucifer out of Paradise. Lucifer, in his pride, had believed that he was greater than God and had challenged the Almighty for possession of Paradise. Pride brought Lucifer down and the Archangel Michael casts him out of Paradise. Wolfram wants to put us in mind of Perceval's sin — the pride that created his fiery independence. Like Lucifer, Perceval's pride will also result in a fall of epic proportions.

Armour prevents recognition. The armour of the Red Knight subsumed Perceval's identity. Armour protects, and we too have our own suit of armour, which we call our identity. We are not born doctors or teachers or shopkeepers. We are not born consumers or householders, rich or poor. What are we without these labels? What are we when the armour of assumed identity is removed and we stand naked? The wise man smiles knowingly. Post-Modernist Man, he says, does not have a single identity but a thousand, waking up each morning and re-inventing himself in accordance with the popular mood. Underneath the mask, we are told, there is nothing that we may call the self.

This is a philosophy of despair and an excuse for cowardice.

Continue to follow Stonehill toward Parrock Hill. Ahead we see two hills and the combe of Whitcombe between the two hills. Here, beneath the earth, lie the remains of a medieval village. We will be climbing the hill to the right. Stonehill lane is only a few hundred paces long, but the high hedges to either side preclude a view to right or left and keep our thoughts focussed on the ascent ahead. The containment of our vision is a useful discipline and will make the vast panorama that is shortly to open before us special.

When we reach the 'T' junction at Kembers Hill (B) we cross the road, veering slightly left and continue in the same direction up the sunken, cobbled track on the opposite side of the road, to the open hillside. Overgrown with a canopy of bushes, this cobbled way serves as an antechamber to the hill beyond and narrows our focus still further before the view finally starts to open out.

This ancient track is broad and even at this point, making for relaxed and meditative walking. This, undoubtedly was an ancient road to Camelot and we may imagine that it was along here that Arthur rode out in search of the Red Knight.

Suddenly, magnificently, and long before we reach the crest of Parrock Hill the panorama explodes outwards. On a clear day, magnificent views of the whole of Somerset and much of Dorset and Wiltshire — Arthur's Kingdom — will be at your feet, including superb views of Cadbury Castle and Glastonbury Tor. With morning or evening light the ramparts of Camelot are sharply defined and the magnificence of the defences will be apparent.

Below us, according to legend, the battle of Camlann was fought on the plain of the River Cam. From that battlefield, the dying Arthur was taken by boat across the flooded moor to Avalon. Sit for a while and picture the vision. See the dark sails and the vague wispy outlines of the Queens who came to bear Arthur to his place of healing.

Beyond the Tor — and from here you really do get the sense of the power of lines of energy — you will see the equally mysterious Brent Knoll, crowned with an Iron Age fort, close by the Severn Sea. Camelot, the Tor and Brent Knoll stand like three giant sentinels guarding the Land of the Celts, the Arthurian kingdom of Dumnonia. We may imagine, in the dark days of the Saxon invasions, the beacon fires blazing on each of these hills, warning the Romano-Celtic populace to prepare to repulse the invader.

Chance will bring Arthur and his court close to where we stand. The camp of bright pavilions will rise close to where Perceval sleeps. That night there is an unseasonable fall of snow and Perceval woke up to a white landscape.

In Chretien de Troye's 'Perceval' and Wolfram's 'Parzival', Arthur's falcon attacked a flock of geese. One of the birds was slightly injured and landed in the snow. When it recovered and flew off it left blood staining the snow. Perceval had observed the incident and ran to the place where the goose had landed:

"When he saw the disturbed snow where the goose had lain and the blood that was visible around it, he leant on his lance to gaze at this sight; for the blood and the snow together have for him the appearance of the fresh colouring on his beloved's face. By these thoughts, he became carried away; for in her face the flush of crimson on her white skin resembled the appearance of these three drops of blood on the snow. As he continued to gaze he thought, to his delight, that he saw the fresh complexion of his fair love's face." [6]

Lost in a reverie of remembrance of Blancheflor, his Queen, Perceval cannot take his eyes from the drops of blood. As Arthur's camp roused itself, the alarm is raised against the lone knight who appeared to be waiting to joust with whomsoever will challenge him. Sagramors was the first to plead with Arthur for permission to break a lance with the mysterious knight but is easily thrown from his horse by Perceval's assault. Sir Kay followed and is likewise defeated. Perceval took his gaze from the drops of blood in the snow just long enough to unhorse his opponents and send them bruised and broken-boned back to Arthur.

"Perceval was prompted by his loyal affection to find the three blood-drops on the snow that had robbed him of his wits. His thoughts concerning the Grail and this semblance of the Queen both afflicted him sorely, but now love weighed heavier in the scales." [7]

Perceval's spiritual quest is forgotten. Love for his queen overshadows his yearning for the Grail.

The tale of the three drops of blood speaks of the predominance of the physical over the spiritual at this moment in Perceval's life. The yearnings of flesh and spirit *should* be in balance but they are not. Eros — sexual love — has become separate from Agape — the unconditional spiritual love of one person for another, which is characterised in Christian symbolism by the self-sacrifice of the Cross. The predominance of erotic love at this moment in Perceval's life makes him a man in the modern sense.

Chastity triumphs in 'Le Morte D'Arthur' and the 'High History of the Holy Grail', and in these later tales the lusty hero of Wolfram and Chretien — who *is* a man — becomes a *thing* of the spirit, made worthy of the Grail by a denial of the desires of the flesh. In the 'High History of the Grail' it is the virginity of Galahad and Perceval — their innocence of the vagina — that made them worthy of the Grail. Lancelot is denied that vision of the Eternal because of his adultery with Guinevere. Underneath these later versions of the Grail myth the old Eve story nags away at our subconscious. The blood and the snow no longer conjures female flesh and the blood of first coitus, but drops of blood from the chalice of the Grail — the blood of salvation symbolized in the Cup of the Last Supper:

"And he thought he saw three angels where before he had seen but two, and there in the centre of the Grail he thought he saw the shape of a child. The foremost knight cried out to Sir Gawain, but he, looking before him, saw three drops of blood drip on to the table, and was so captivated by the sight that he did not say a word. And so the maidens passed on by, leaving the knights looking at one another in dismay. Sir Gawain could not take his eyes off the three drops of blood, but when he tried to kiss them they moved away from him..." [8]

The ancient undercurrent of the vessel that bleeds and gives birth to hope persists. Jessie Weston was one of the first to argue that the Grail Quest is a cipher for the masculine yearning for the ecstasy of the vagina. C.G.Jung popularized the idea of the Grail as a feminine archetype, counterbalancing the values of a medieval society that blamed Eve for all our woes and made virginity the ideal state for womankind. From where we stand the Virgin theme is, according to Maltwood, written in the landscape beneath our feet. As we gaze north west toward Glastonbury, the busy A303 and Fosse Way (A37) mark out the land in which the star sign, Virgo, is defined in the landscape by the River Cary and Dyke Brook. A lyrical post-war writer, Lt. Col Harwood Steele, MC, describes the scene from Camelot, which he advised visitors to climb to appreciate the "6000 yard giant":

"...Come with me, 500 feet up Castle Hill, to gaze over the 'forbidden Land of Logres', and drink in the mystery and enchantment of this 'Cauldron of Wisdom', whilst the sun sinks down into the western sea only to rise again as King Arthur in a golden dawn." [9]

Sir Kay returned from his joust in a bad way. His arm was broken and his collar-bone dislocated. Finally, Gawain asked permission to approach the brooding knight. Unlike the others, Gawain suggested to Arthur that the knight should be treated with courtesy:

"The knight is brooding over some loss he's suffered, or his love has been stolen from him. But if that were your pleasure, I would go to see if he has come out of his reverie and beg him to come here to you." [10]

Arthur gave his consent. Gawain approached Perceval and noted the direction of his gaze toward the drops of blood. Rather than challenge him, Gawain threw a cape of Syrian silk over the blood and Perceval's reverie was broken. The courteous Gawain is then able to engage the Red Knight in conversation. So pleasing was Gawain's manner to Perceval that they became fast friends there and then — a friendship that would ultimately take them both to the attainment of the Grail. Gawain was soon able to persuade Perceval to present himself before King Arthur.

Arthur and his court rejoiced at finding Perceval, whose heroic deeds and good looks are already the talk of the land. Having achieved their objective, the camp was struck and the court headed back for Camelot. We will join this merry train, with its loaded mules, laughing, mischievous pages, pipes, and tumbrels and glittering knights with their deer hounds and falcons ready on their gloves and gossiping ladies in their finery trailing behind. The day is bright and there is the promise of a stag or two as we wind our way to Camelot.

Continue following the well-defined track toward Corton Ridge.

In time, you will come to a field boundary, where two fences meet to form a 'V' (C). Go through the gate and continue on the bridleway to a second field boundary. Go through and continue along the path for a further 300 metres. Follow the Right of Way as it switches back to Sutton Montis, sloping gently down the hill the way we have come.

Go through the gate (D) and follow the line of the bridleway (less obvious now), toward the large oak trees in the lower corner of the field. Here there is a stile and waymarks directing us from the Right of Way indicated on the OS map to follow a track due west down the hill to join the lane that goes directly to Corton Wood Farm (E). From Corton Wood Farm we turn right to follow the lane toward Sutton Farm (F). Continue straight on for Sutton Farm and Sutton Montis. Walk past the small red brick cottage on the right to the road junction, where an old signpost directs us into the village.

The hill of Camelot with its bare, flat summit plateau rises dramatically ahead, dominating the village. From here you can see the South West Gate of Camelot.

Local legend has it that on St. John's Eve at Midsummer, you can hear the hoof-beats of the horses of King Arthur and his knights as they ride down from Camelot to drink at a spring beside Sutton Montis Church. [11]

Leading from the South West Gate in a northerly direction toward Glastonbury is an ancient track, now all but lost, called King Arthur's Hunting Causeway. Tales were told until recent times of wild rides along this track on stormy nights when King Arthur, with his knights and hounds following the chase, thundered along the causeway to the distant Tor.

Pause at the beautiful little church **(G)** at the end of the village and imagine the churchyard echoing to the neighing of horses and the clatter of hooves as the ghost knights wheel their horses about the spring before heading north to hunt the stag and the boar to Avalon.

*Continue along the road out of the village for about 500 metres. Where the road takes a sharp left **(H)** we turn right through a field gate, where a part concealed 'Leland Trail' sign indicates a public footpath to South Cadbury. Follow the field boundary to the left for about fifty metres and cross the stile to continue the footpath route. We follow the field boundary in a straight line toward South Cadbury, crossing three stiles in all, until we come to Folly Lane. Shortly thereafter, the same direction brings us into South Cadbury and the Red Lion pub **(I)**, situated at the crossroads in the centre of the village.* The pub welcomes walkers and is an excellent place to take your ease before ascending to the magical fort of Camelot.

From the Red Lion turn right and walk to the church. Just past the church turn right into Castle Lane to ascend to the North East Gate of Camelot. The lower part of the path can be muddy in autumn and winter but is usually dry and firm higher up. It is necessary to go through two kissing gates on your ascent.

Shortly after the second kissing gate the track is crossed by a path following the line of one of the ramparts that encircles the fort. To the left you will find a cattle trough. Just before it, emerging from the bank of the rampart is a small well, covered with a small arch made out of a single block of stone. This is King Arthur's Well. Tradition has it that on the night of the full moon, Arthur and his knights ride round the camp with silver-shod horses and water their steeds at this well. Sadly, the well shaft is now filled with leaves and debris. Once upon a time, it was said that the shaft led deep into the hollow hill. Someone shouting into King Arthur's Well could be heard in Queen Anne's Wishing-Well on the other side of the hill. Those wishing to put the legend to the test are warned that Queen Anne's Wishing-Well is difficult to locate and the paths to it are overgrown or torn up by grazing cattle.

We now return to the main path from King Arthur's Well and continue upward to the summit plateau.

Imagine as you walk up the cobbled track, the glittering spectacle of Arthur's return. A squire holds the bridle of the prancing warhorse that carries the youthful Perceval. Relieved of his red armour, he is clothed in robes of brocade of Nineveh, adorned with a girdle of precious stones and an emerald brooch given to him by Cunneware, a maiden whose honour he had defended when she was insulted by Sir Kay.

Around him, beautiful maidens laugh and blush as they catch the glance of this most dazzling of men. Fellow knights look on enviously at the youth that has bested the best of them, including, Sir Kay, who nurses a broken arm and leg. Arthur himself leads Perceval by the hand. As we reach the green fields that crown Camelot, Perceval is greeted by Guinevere and honoured with a kiss.

Banners and pennants surround the plain, each bearing the arms of the hearth companions and liege men who have united under Arthur's dragon banner to defeat the Saxon horde. War drums startle the crows to flight and they wheel and caw above. Pipes and song accompany the tumbling jester and mingle with the cries of sellers of silk and trinkets of gold and bronze to please the ladies. The smells of roasting sucking pig, venison, and fowl caught by fine falcons that very morning fill the air and whet the appetite. The saddle cup is offered to the thirsty knights and a cheer raised to the return of the Red Knight....

All this was long ago and a few broken stones are all that remain of the glory of old. A cow sneers at our dreams as it tramples a fragment of bronze filigree that once adorned the girdle of a queen.

To our right, we see the remains of the stone rampart that once crowned this fort. *We can choose to wander freely about the fort but it is better to follow the wall at least as far as the South West Gate (J)*. Keep your eyes open for the gaps between the trees that give a view of the Tor. As we walk along the remains of the Saxon wall we note the stones that break through the ground, a sad remnant of lost ages of warrior heroes and their legendary deeds. Camelot's story is not of one heroic age but many. More than one hundred and fifty generations separate the first occupants of this fort from the last. No doubt, there were periods of silence on this hill during those long centuries, when, like today, cattle hooves and plough unearth the faces of the past from the iron dust.

As we walk toward the South West Gate, the impressive nature of the fort becomes apparent. Even now, with the ramparts broken and worn down, it is no mean feat to scale these defenses from the fields below. With the ramparts faced with stone and topped with a palisade of stout timbers, it would have taken a very determined enemy to force their way in.

Looking northwest, we see the Tor guarding the hills on which the town and abbey of Glastonbury are built. Camelot is one of the finest places to appreciate the magic of Glastonbury and the leap of the spirit that the pilgrim of old must have felt when they first sighted St. Michael's Tower crowning that most famous hill. On cold mornings mist lies on the levels like a lake and Glastonbury is an island once more. Watch the sunset from here, where Briton and Saxon warrior alike stood each in his own time against the invading horde, and your heart will leap with a yearning for the soul of all that is Avalon. This marvelous view of the seven isles of Avalon puts us in mind of the poem of Taliesin — possibly the earliest written survival of the Arthurian Grail Quest — which accords so well with this landscape. Was it from here, as the Welsh poet Taliesin recounts, that Arthur set off with three shiploads of his hearth companions to seek the Cauldron amongst the seven sacred islands and of whom but seven returned?

"Since my song resounded in the turning Caer,
I am pre-eminent. My first song
Was of the Cauldron itself.
Nine maidens kindled it with their breath —
Of what nature was it?
Pearls were about its rim,
It would not boil a coward's portion.
Lleminawg thrust his flashing sword
Deep within it;
And before dark gates, a light was lifted.

When we went with Arthur — a mighty labour —
Save only seven, none returned from Caer Fedwydd." [12]

Glastonbury provides us with seven sacred islands, which once would have been more apparent when Glastonbury was surrounded by water and these places would indeed have been islands in a sea of treacherous marsh. By medieval times, each was crowned with a chapel. They provide us with a landscape that matches the Quest voyage of Arthur and his men in Taliesin's Preiddeu Annwn, ending at Caer Siddi, or Ynis Vitris the Isle of Glass — the Celtic name for the Island of Avalon.

King Edgar's charter of the tenth century lists the islands alongside Glastonbury, Isle of Avalon: The charter names them as "Bekaria quae parva Hibernia dicitur, Godeneia, Marteneseia, Ferramere, Padenaberga et Andredeseia."In English, these are Beckery, or Little Ireland, Godney or God's Island, Martinsea or Marchey, Ferramere or Mere, Panborough, and Andrewsea or Nyland. In the days of Taliesin hermits occupied each island.

In a little while the wall drops away and there is a distinct gap in the defences. This is the South West Gate. Beneath us are the houses, orchards, farms, and gardens of Sutton Montis. We are at the spot where the ghost of Arthur and his companions leave the fort to hunt the stag and ride the causeway that joins Camelot to the Isle of Avalon. That this causeway no longer exists adds to its mystery — it is a ghost path, accessible only to the dead. When the South West Gate was excavated by Leslie Alcock in 1970 he made a gruesome discovery. The scattered bones of thirty men, women, and children were uncovered, accompanied by a large number of roman pikes and javelins. The bodies appeared to have been thrown out onto the road and left for animals to scatter and dismember. These bones are all that remain of the victims of a massacre carried out by the Romans when they seized the fort from the Celts. Some time after the massacre the Romans returned to destroy the defences and the timber gate was burned and toppled over their pitiful remains. [13]

It was only when the Romans had left, leaving the Britons defenceless, that Arthur rose to build Camelot on this hill so that he and his knights might be a wall to his people.

Cross the South West Gate and continue your walk along the walls of Camelot. Soon you will be gazing across to Parrock Hill and Whitcombe, where our walk had taken us earlier in the day. From here, turn left to walk toward the centre of the fort, along the ridge that dominates the plateau, to the topograph built to celebrate the Millennium. This topograph indicates the direction of places associated with Arthurian Romance. It gives, for example, the direction of Tintagel Castle in Cornwall, Arthur's legendary birthplace.

The topograph stands above the foundations the Feasting Hall of Arthurian times and if the Round Table ever existed it was on this spot that Arthur and his knights met and pledged their lives to the Quest for the Grail.

Concealed by the earth at your feet are the post-holes of a feasting hall, some sixty-three by thirty-four feet in size. In one of these holes were found the sherds of a wine-jar from Mediterranean regions which date to the Arthurian period. Similar sherds have been found at Tintagel castle, and reflect the fact that the drinking of imported Mediterranean wines survived the departure of the Romans amongst the Romano-Celtic nobility of Arthur's time. [14]

Arthur and his chosen hearth companions of the Table Round are entering the Feasting Hall that your imagination has raised around you. Horns bray and drums raise a cacophany as Arthur and his knights stand at their places and their squires and pages relieve them of their arms. Perceval is invited to take his place at the Table Round for the first time, having proved himself worthy of his peers. That empty place — the Siege Perilous — is filled and the Companionship of the Round Table is complete. The knights will drink and carouse from sunset to the break of day. When they have taken their rest, there are tournaments, tales from the bards and merriment from the jesters. Each man has his cup filled with joy almost as if an invisible Grail gave each a foretaste of its delights.

Alas, too briefly! The celebrations had lasted barely twenty-four hours when they were interrupted by the foul apparition of the loathely maid.

> "They spent the whole night in celebration and the following day too before, on the next day, they saw a damsel approaching on a tawny mule, holding a whip in her right hand...."

The description that follows of the hideous maid sends shivers down the spine. The half-forgotten myths from the days of the Celts reach from the distant past and plant this dark creature into the heart of the Grail story. Dressed in fine fabric of Ghent, bluer than azure, and a hat of peacock feathers lined with cloth-of-gold, her finery could not hide her ugliness:

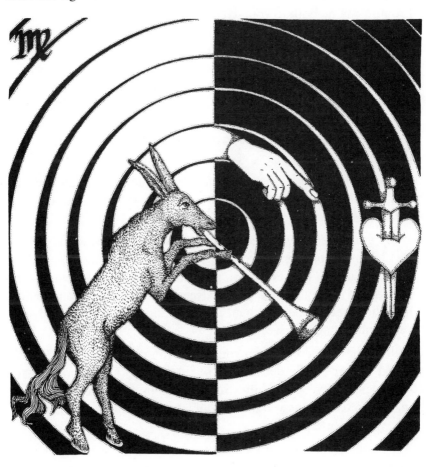

"A plait of hair fell down over the hat and dangled on her mule — it was long, black, tough, about as soft as a boar's bristles. Her nose was like a dog's and to the length of several spans a pair of tusks jutted from her jaws. Both eyebrows pushed past her hair-band and drooped down in tresses. Cundrie's ears resembled a bear's. This fetching sweetheart had hands the colour of ape-skin. Seldom were lances broken for her love." [15]

Perceval, having just won his place at the Round Table and admired by all, is brought down by this monstrous vision. In his moment of glory, he is reminded before the whole court of his failure to ask the question of the Grail and the suffering that failure has wrought. Cundrie speaks to Arthur first:

"O son of King Utpandragun, what you have done today has brought shame both to yourself and to many a Briton. The Round Table is destroyed: dishonour has been joined to it...."She turned and spoke directly to Parzival. "Cursed be the beauty of your face! I am less of a monster than you. Parzival, speak up! Tell why, when the sorrowful Fisherman sat there, you did not relieve him of his sighs? By your silence you acquired great sin. May your tongue now become as empty as your heart is empty of right feeling. O Munsalvaesche, sorrows home! To comfort you, alas, there now is none!" [15]

Because of his actions, she continued, the Fisher King's lands would be laid waste, knights killed, wives made widows and children orphaned.

"By your silence you acquired a great sin...You saw the Grail carried into your presence, the keen knives of silver and the Bloody Lance! You ender of joy, donor of sorrow! Had you thought of asking there at Munsalvaesche, your Question would have brought you more than Tabronit, city of fabled wealth in heathendom, could give." [16]

Cundrie, the Sorceress, then rode from the circle, leaving Perceval shamed by her public declaration of his failure. The women of the court began to weep for him. Some of them attempted to console him, but Perceval knew that he could not be happy again until he finds what is lost:

"I shall never own myself happy till I have seen the Gral, whether the time be short or long. My thoughts impel me to that goal, from which nothing shall sever me to the end of my days. Pray advise me, gentlemen, how to win your good will. Dire execution has been done on me here with words, nor do I reproach any whose favour I have lost. Because of that I am in great haste to take my leave of you. Whilst my reputation flourished you all gave me your company. I now declare you free till I have gained the thing the lack of which has seared my verdant joy! Great sorrow will attend me such as brings heart's rain to eyes...For whatever marvels men have storied of, the Gral has more! Its lord drags out a wretched life. — Helpless Anfortas, what help was it to you when I was at your side?" [17]

As Perceval is about to depart, Gawain offers him his comfort and support. In his parting words Perceval not only turns away from the court of Arthur, but from God Himself, thus venturing into the world entirely and completely alone:

"Alas, what is God? Were He all-powerful — were God active in His almightiness — He would not have brought us to such shame! Ever since I knew of Grace I have been His humble servitor. But now I quit his service." [18]

Perceval was hailed as one of the greatest knights in the world. He had defeated the best of the Round Table, who were the foremost knights of the age. His rise has been meteoric — and so was his fall. Shamed before his peers for his failure to ask the question of the Fisher King and relieving the Grail King of his agony, Perceval has no choice but to turn his back on the honours heaped upon him and enter the Waste Land.

It is time to leave. We too must follow Perceval's lonely path of the Grail Quest. The joy that was his but an hour ago is gone. Shamed before the whole court he knows that only the Grail can restore him. He is a man in search of his soul. Hubris has brought him to this pass — in which he sought false glory in the armour of another. He began as a man without a name and assumed the name and the values of another. It is what we all do. And when we have those rare moments of stillness and freedom from following the path that others have chosen for us, we wonder who we are and where we are going. Letting go of our assumed identity is hard — often it leaves a space we feel we shall never fill. But let go we must or live falsely always. To ask the question and find no answer is better than not to ask the question at all. Not to ask the question is to live on the very surface of life. It is the self-same question we shall one day ask of the Grail.

Continue across the field to the North West Gate and return to the village by the same path you ascended. Return slowly and thoughtfully to the village of South Cadbury. Let melancholy thoughts fill you. Acknowledge the emptiness within. This emptiness will drive you on. The companionship of the Round Table — all you have fought for — will be hard to leave. You are leaving the friends you have loved and the values you have fought for. But go with hope. Remember that what the Grail gives is unconditional and eternal. As long as you hold faith it will never desert you. To accomplish the Quest is to fill the vessal of your soul.

1. Alfred Lord Tennyson, The Holy Grail, (from Idylls of the King, Henry S. King &Co, 1875) P266

2. John Leland, quoted by Leslie Alcock in By South Cadbury is that Camelot... , (Book Club Associates, London, 1972) P.11

3. For more detailed information see Leslie Alcock, P.21

4. ibid., P.194

5. Quest del Saint Graal, see The Quest of the Holy Grail, (Penguin Books, 1969) P42

6. Chretien de Troyes, Perceval, trans. D.D.R.Owen, (Everyman edition, J.M..Dent, 1999) P.430

7. Wolfram von Eschenbach, Parzival, written circa 1210, trans. A.T. Hatto, (Penguin Books, 1986), P.155

8. The High Book of the Grail, a translation of the thirteenth-century romance of Perlesvaus, trans. Nigel Bryant, (D.S.Brewer, 1996) P.79

9. Lt. Col Harwood Steele, undated private publication, re-printed in A Glastonbury Reader edit John Matthews, (Aquarian/Thorsons 1993) P.127

10. Chretien de Troyes, P.432

11. For a full account of local legends see J.A. Bennett, Camelot, (Proceedings, Somersetshire Archaeological and Natural History Society, 36 1890, part 2) pp. 1-19

12. Taliesin, The Spoils of Annwn, trans John Matthews (Sources of the Grail, edit. John Matthews, Floris Books 1997) P.31

13. see Leslie Alcock, P104

14. ibid., P.177

14. Wolfram von Eschenbach, P.164

15. ibid., P.164

16. ibid., P.165

17. ibid.,P.171

18. ibid.,P172

The Fifth Quest

The Horn of Capricorn

Gawain and the King of the Wood.

BOUT a mile and a half to the east of Glastonbury is an ancient linear earthwork known as Ponter's Ball. Over twelve feet high and more than a half-mile in length this rampart transects a ridge that joins Avalon to Pennard Hill. When the levels were still lakes and marsh Ponter's Ball defended the only land access to the Isle of Avalon. The A361 Shepton Mallet Road now runs across this narrow isthmus, cutting through the remains of these ancient defences. The age of the monument is something of a mystery. It may well be Iron Age, built at the same time as Glastonbury's Lake Village. Equally, it may be Arthurian, built to defend the sacred isle of the Briton and the birthplace of Christianity from the invading Saxon horde. That it is ancient is certain. Folklore has Arthur's Hunting Causeway, linking Camelot to the Isle of Avalon, crossing Ponter's Ball, although where is no longer clear.

The name is believed to derive from the Latin, *Pontis Vallum*, meaning the 'Wall of the Bridge'. Mary Caine draws our attention to an alternative suggestion, which points out that there is no bridge here, and suggests an Etruscan derivation — 'Puntes Bal', or 'sacrifice of Bel'. [1] I would argue that the bridge in question is the land bridge joining Glastonbury to the high ground to the east and Ponter's Ball is indeed the wall of that bridge. Excavation of a section of the earthwork indicated a ditch that was as much as ten feet deep, creating a bulwark of over twenty feet for the enemy to scale. It is likely that a wooden stockade topped this formidable earth bank. Ponter's Ball lines up with a similar ancient bank and ditch crossing the high ground in Butleigh Wood, known as New Ditch. If the earthwork were to continue beyond this, it would align with the hillfort at Dundon Hill. Philip Rahtz, the archaeologist, speculates that what remains may be fragments of a major defensive structure, which blocked all land access to Avalon. With the age of all three monuments still uncertain, they could be the work of a single Celtic warlord. The true history of Glastonbury will not be known until these important earthworks are properly investigated.

In the Glastonbury Zodiac, this fabulous earthwork is the horn of Capricorn, with its nose pointing toward the Tor and its feet resting against Launcherly Hill. We may speculate, without stretching a point too far, that Ponter's Ball is also a religious monument, separating Ynis Vitris, the Sacred Isle and Gateway to the Underworld, from the land of mortals. That it should also be seen as the horns of a goat is apt. This is the horn of the Earth Sign, a phallic symbol, representing the more elemental dimension of love. I am not suggesting that this is how it was perceived in ancient times — its function as a boundary is transparent — but we shall view it in the same symbolic spirit as Maltwood.

Into this earthy landscape we shall introduce, as indeed Maltwood did, Perceval's Quest partner, Gawain, son of King Lot. In the great tales of Chretien and Wolfram Gawain's adventures parallel those of Perceval, although his weakness for women will often lead him from the Quest. His passion for the fair sex is made apparent in Wolfram's tale:

"Gawan, the glory of the table round, had had experience of such trouble. He had come to know it rudely when he stabbed a knife through his own palm under Love's dominion and that of a noble woman's friendship." [2]

It is not possible to understand Grail Mythology without paying some attention to the issue of courtly love. Having declared his love for a lady a knight was required to prove his devotion by engaging on dangerous quests in her name, to demonstrate that her love meant more to him than life. Knights in Arthurian legend are sometimes mocked and derided by the women they love, who demand unreasonable and often fatal deeds of their paramours.

So it is with Gawain, whose love for Orgeluse, Duchess of Logroys, proved almost fatal. In a tale with its origins in Druidic tradition, she pits him against Gramoflanz, the King of the Wood. Gramoflanz was also responsible for the wound in the thigh borne by Anfortas, the Grail King, which had left him in great pain and his country a waste land. It is the wound delivered by this Winter King that created a desolate kingdom that cannot renew itself. Gawain will be asked to bring a wreath from the wood — believed to represent a wreath of mistletoe — clearing the way for the defeat of the Oak King and the return of spring to the winter land.

It was an ancient belief that the life of the oak tree was sustained in the mistletoe during the winter months, for whilst the tree was dead, the mistletoe remained green and alive. Primitive man sought to preserve his gods by keeping them poised between heaven and earth. So it is with the divine mistletoe, which remains forever held above the earth and beneath the heavens. When cut from the tree, however, the thread of life is cut too, making it possible for the Holly King to begin his rule.

It is in the spirit of the struggle between Gawain and the Oak King that we will visit Glastonbury's oldest trees — the ancient oaks of Gog and Magog, where once stood an entire Druid grove of ancient oaks. The tale is rooted in the power and reverence bestowed on such ancient trees in the Age of the Druid, when the abode of the gods was the Oak Grove, the essence of which Grail legend preserves. The tree theme is emphasised by the many orchards we will pass on our walk.

Without doubt Spring and blossom-time will bring the greatest visual rewards. Like Queen Guinevere we may go a-Maying. Alternatively, early Autumn will bring the quieter delights of trees heavy with fruit.

Today we will make our own journey to the East. In doing so we will walk upon the Horn of Capricorn and reflect upon the power of love in our own lives. We will continue on our pilgrim Quest to its culmination at the two sacred oaks — Gog and Magog, to pray for healing and reconciliation with our memories of love lost and love unfulfilled. Our walk will take us from below Chalice Well Gardens by way of Cinnamon Lane, to fields devoted to orchard and pasture on the southern shores of the isle of Avalon. We will cross Ponter's Ball and then turn north to touch the northern tip of the earthwork at Havyatt Farm. From there we will walk in the general direction of the Tor, following the snout of Capricorn to Norwood Park. After walking up Stone Down Lane and visiting the ancient oaks, Gog and Magog, we will return to our starting point.

The Horn of Capricorn

If you have a vehicle you can park it at the Rural Life Museum and begin your day with a tour of the museum and a visit to their pleasant café. Alternatively, you can start in the centre of Glastonbury, which will add a few minutes to your walk.

From the Rural Life Museum, follow the busy Shepton Mallet road away from the town, past Chalice Well Gardens, until you reach the first turning on the right. Here we dive down Cinnamon Lane to escape the traffic. Thankfully, your next encounter with the A361 will be simply to cross it at Havyatt, a mile or so up the road.

Cinnamon Lane is invariably quiet and the stroll along the road is always a pleasure. You will soon have expansive views across Kennard Moor toward the village of Baltonsborough in the middle distance. We begin with a grassy playground to our left and a little later a pleasant apple orchard, crowned with a dramatic view of the Tor high above. This is the first orchard of many which we will encounter in this 'Orchard Isle' landscape.

At Lower Edgarley Farm, where Cinnamon Lane turns sharp left, we leave the road (B). Just after the farmhouse is a five-barred gate to the

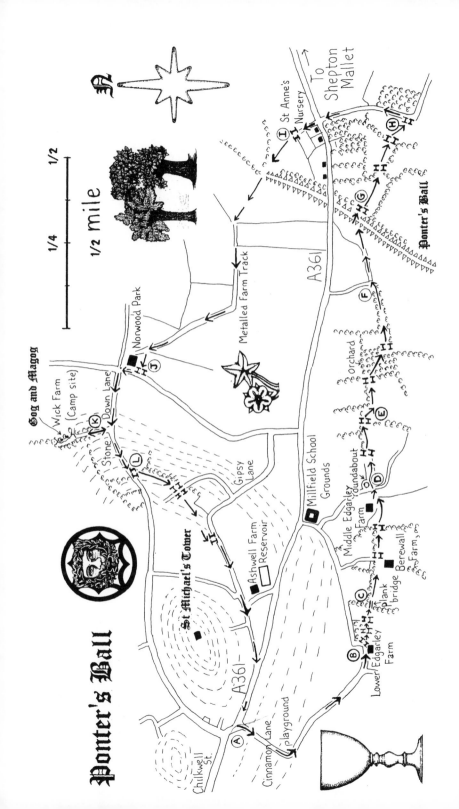

Ponter's Ball

St Michael's Tower

Gog and Magog

Wick Farm (Camp site)

Norwood Park

St Anne's Nursery

To Shepton Mallet

Ponter's Ball

1/4   1/2   1/2

1/2 mile

N

A361

Metalled Farm Track

Down Lane

Stone

Gipsy Lane

Ashwell Farm Reservoir

Millfield School Grounds

Middle Edgarley Farm

Edgarley Roundabout

Berewall Farm

Plank bridge

Lower Edgarley Farm

orchard

Chilkwell St.

Cinnamon Lane

playground

A   B   C   D   E   F   G   H   I   J   K   L

right and a 'public footpath' sign. Go through the gate and cross the stile a few metres further on. Follow the apple orchard boundary to your left until you come to another stile. Cross the stile and the field following the same easterly direction.

It was through a green meadow such as this that Gawain was riding when he glimpsed the aftermath of combat. A shield, holed by a lance thrust hung from the bough of a tree and to the shield was tethered a palfrey, harnessed for a lady.

Gawain pondered if this was some lady knight that might give him the pleasure of a joust or a wrestling match. His sexual fantasies soon ended as he rode closer. A distraught woman was sat amidst the clover, cradling the head of a wounded knight in her lap. The knight was dying, bleeding internally and barely able to breathe. Gawain dismounted and showed his battlefield experience in saving the man. Cutting a thin branch from a tree, he trimmed off the bark to make a tube. He inserted the tube into the chest wound and then instructed the women to suck until the blood started to pour out of the wound. With the pressure off his heart the knight recovered from his swoon and soon revived.

The knight told Gawain that Lischoys Gwelljus had wounded him. Vowing revenge on the knight's behalf, Gawain followed the trail of blood until he saw a castle in the distance. The castle belonged to Clinschor, the magician.

*On the other side of the field, the fence curves in and undergrowth partly conceals the stile from view (**C**). At the time of writing, a single strand of barbed wire obstructs the public footpath at this point, probably to keep the cattle from trampling the area around the stile. This can be easily ducked under. Cross the stile and the little plank bridge on the other side and follow the field boundaries to your left to Bere Wall (Berewall) Farm.*

The instructions may seem a little complicated but do not despair. As the map reveals we are walking almost directly east and the instructions are simply to aid locating stiles. Do locate the stiles, however, as the hedges almost invariably conceal deep rhynes full of muddy water. Underfoot it can be a little boggy after rain, but in summer, it makes for delightful, easy walking. For us this landscape will become the Duchy of Logroys and the Tor shall stand for the Castle of Clinschor, the evil magician. The description given by Wolfram fits the Tor remarkably well!

"The structure of the castle was splendid! With its path ascending in spirals the castle hill resembled a top, so that when a simple person saw it from a way off he thought it was spinning round! All round the castle hill ran a palisade of cultivated trees — figs, pomegranites, olives, as well as vines and other productive plants, all growing in abundance." [3]

It is on the way to the castle that Gawain chanced upon the fair Orgeluse.

"From the rock there leapt a spring, beside which — and this did not displease him — was a fair lady. He gazed at her with delight despite himself, she was the fairest flower of all feminine beauty.... She was of radiant charm, shapely, refined. Her name was Orgeluse de Logroys, and the story tells of her that she was a lure to love's desire, sweet balm to a man's eyes, windlass to his heartstrings." [4]

Gawain was quick to declare his affections but he was just as quickly rebuffed:

"If you desire my love, what have you done to deserve it of me? Trundle your wretched desires at other loves than mine. If you are a man who serves for love, if thirst for adventure has brought you out to do deeds of arms to win a lady's favour, you will find no reward in me!" [5]

Orgeluse sent the love-struck knight to fetch her palfrey from a nearby orchard. Gawain found knights and ladies gathered, courtiers of the fair Orgeluse. Some warned Gawain, with tears and entreaties, that his service to their lady would do him no good at all. He ignored their advice and took the palfrey to Orgeluse. Mounting the horse, she bad him follow and continued to insult him as they journeyed across orchard and heath, gay with flowers. Her insults are compounded by a trick carried out by a servant of Orgeluse, resulting in the loss of his horse, and forcing him to ride on a sorry old nag, lame in all four legs and with a rotting saddle of felt. Gawain considered the beauty of Orgeluse as adequate compensation for the insults and humiliation she heaped on him:

"He found her well-salted jibes so acceptable that he did not mind what she said, since whenever he looked at her he was quit of any pain she caused him. In his eyes she was May-time in person, a blossoming that outshone all things bright — sweetness to his eye, yet bitterness to his heart." [6]

As we continue on our path to Berewall we shall imagine ourselves in the train of this haughty duchess on her white palfrey, with Gawain riding a sorry nag and looking every inch a fool following behind. She smiles and mocks, knowing the power of her beauty to melt men's hearts and turn them into fools — before leading them to their deaths. We too must reflect on the times that Mistress Love has turned us into fools. How many times has love led to an insufferable

loss? To find the Grail we must seize hold of the power that only love can give and use it to pierce our souls. For there, and there alone, will we find the Temple of the Grail.

Berewall Farm is now accommodation for Millfield School, which we will see more of later. To the left of the white-painted farmhouse, a stile takes you on to the next stage of the footpath. After Berewall follow, the northern field boundary until you come to a five-barred gate. Go through the gate and then cross the next field, aiming for the farm buildings in the top left-hand corner by Middle Edgarley Farm. This field can be a little boggy in winter months or after heavy rain. Negotiating the route around the farm is a touch complicated. A concreted track runs to the side of the barn (D). Cross the stile to the right of the five-barred gate on the opposite side of the track to the barn. Aim for the metal gate twenty-five metres further on in the top far corner of the small field. The stile is to the right of the gate. Bear left from here up a grassy lane to a roundabout in the school grounds. Keep to the right of the grounds until you come to a public footpath sign on a post and follow the pleasant grassy track past the Millfield School playing fields. Follow the top left hedge-line of the next field until you reach the hedge on the far side. At the time of writing a battered five-barred gate bars the way and cannot be opened (E). It is necessary to climb over this gate. From the gate the path follows the top of the field to another stile after which we enter an orchard. The Right of Way crosses the orchard diagonally to join a track at the bottom corner of the field.

Orgeluse led Gawain through a forest. The castle that he had seen before from a distance reappeared. Gawain has never see the like before, so magnificent were its many turrets, towers and battlements. At its windows stood many beautiful ladies. The Duchess had brought Gawain to the castle of Clinschor, the magician, with deliberate intent, for Gawain was to face a great danger within its walls.

We must imagine the countryside as it was at the time of Arthur to make the tale fit:

> "A causeway led to a broad, fast-flowing navigable river, and he and his lady rode towards it. Beside the quay, there was a meadow where much jousting was done. The fortress loomed above the river." [7]

We must imagine the Brue in flood as our river. Having led him to this point Orgeluse summoned the ferry-boat, and much to Gawain's chagrin, departs.

Gawain is promptly attacked by Lischois Gwelljus, the same young, vigorous knight, who had wounded the knight whose life Gawain had saved earlier. A fierce fight ensued. Gawain fought at a disadvantage, given the weakness of his mount, and both men end up on their backs amidst the meadow flowers. With shield and sword the fight continued, with sparks flying and shields steadily reduced to splinters. The young knight is almost a match for Gawain. The reason for his ferocity became apparent once Gawain has defeated him and demanded his surrender. He too is in love with Orgeluse:

> "Rather than surrender I offer my life. Let your noble hand make an end of whatever fame I knew, for I am accurst in the eyes of God who is oblivious of my glory! For love of Orgeluse the noble Duchess many worthy men have had to yield their fame to me, so that you can inherit more fame by slaying me." [8]

In defeating the man who defeated all others none had a stronger claim than Gawain to the affections of Orgeluse. This encounter proved fortuitous twice over, for this knight had won Gawain's stolen warhorse in a previous encounter, and, having won the fight Gawain reclaimed his mount.

Gawain spared the man and spent the night in the abode of the ferryman. In the morning, the ferryman spoke of the strange land Gawain has entered. He discovered that he has entered Terre Marveile, the Country of Marvels. The castle is Schastel Marveile, in which four hundred maidens are imprisoned. No knight has survived its perils. Only by facing the perils of the Lit Marveile can the country be rid of evil. The ferryman also informed Gawain that he carried a great knight across the river only the day before:

> "His shield bears the scars of many jousts. He was riding here in quest of the Gral." [9]

From this description, Gawain realised that he is hard on the heels of Perceval. Now he knows that he is moving closer to the heart of the Grail Quest. The challenge Gawain must face before continuing on the Quest had not been asked of Perceval, who passed through the country without making enquiry of the Schastel Marveile. No longer embroiled in the pursuit of love or fame Perceval, single-mindedly pursued the only thing that can give a man his heart's desire. He had ridden away from all the temptations that Orgeluse had put in his way. For Gawain, the desire for women and fame is still irresistable.

When the farm track turns sharp left (F) go through the gate where a public footpath sign directs us to Kennard Moor Drove. Follow the track that runs to the top left of the field until you come to the long low bank of Ponter's Ball.

Enjoy this magnificent earthwork, built not to provide the horns of a goat but to defend Avalon from attack by land, crossing this narrow isthmus from marsh to marsh. Avalon's island status is not entirely prehistoric. As late as 1873 the Tor was reached by floodwater and 107 square miles of Somerset were under water from October to March. In 1960 a very wet October and November all but made Glastonbury an island again. One argument against the antiquity of the Glastonbury Zodiac is that, if it is as old as Maltwood and Mary Caine claim (5000 years), its makers would have been working on a number of key sections of the design under water! I digress. The Glastonbury Zodiac is a matter of the heart not the head and the archaeology of the wetlands should not be allowed to mar our journey across this Sea of Dreams.

Before you leave Ponter's Ball, look back the way you have come and enjoy the splendid panorama of Avalon, the heart of the Grail Legend and the sweep of the Mendips beyond, where Joseph of Arimathea trod, accompanied by the boy Jesus. We stand on a sacred boundary. Beyond it lies the Kingdom of Prester John, the Avalon of Arthur and the Munsalvesche of Wolfram on which stands the Grail castle. However despoiled it may be by the works of modernity, the heart beneath the earth remains intact. Ahead of us lie the earthly terrors of Schastel Marveile!

The mysterious ferryman has taken Gawain into a land of marvels that is not quite of this world. He has come to a hill that seems from a distance to spin like a top and now he is about to enter the strange and marvellous castle.

The roots of this tale are ancient. Celtic myth speaks of the faerie king who lives within the spinning castle, who guards the gate to another world. The motifs are simple enough to interpret. This is a journey to the Underworld, the crossing of the boundary between life and death. The journey across water with the ferryman is a simple image of death. To face death in this way is one of the challenges that each Quest knight must face. Only this time, should the brave knight prevail, he will be able to cross the barrier of death and return to the world of the living.

At the heart of the castle is a chamber in which lies a magnificent bed, the Lit Marveile. As if ordained by magic it is the first room that Gawain encounters on entering the castle. Opulently decorated, the floor is of polished jasper, chysolite, and sardine. In order to free all those who lie imprisoned in the castle Gawain must spend a night in that bedchamber:

> "The pavement was so glassy that Gawan could hardly find purchase for his feet. As often as he made a step, the Bed moved on from where it was. He took a flying jump and landed plumb in the middle. No one will ever hear again of the speed at which the Bed went crashing from side to side! Not one wall did it spare, but hurtled against each so that the whole Castle echoed with its thuds." [10]

So overwhelmed was Gawain by the din, that he pulled his shield over himself. It was to save his life for shortly thereafter he was showered with thousands of stones and crossbow bolts. Had he not leapt on the bed in his armour he surely would have perished. Such was the power of the assault that many bolts and stones cut and bruised him through his chain mail. At last the assault stopped.

No sooner had he recovered and begun to cut the crossbow bolts from his shield than a door opened and a lion as big as a horse leapt in. After a struggle that left the bed chamber covered in blood, Gawain finally killed his foe. The battle was over and some of the maidens of the castle came to attend to his wounds.

Gawain is left seriously injured by the night's events and his fifty wounds are bathed and bandaged by the maidens. He is treated with a special salve that has been brought from Munsalvaesche, and his heart lifted at the mention of that name. It was not potent enough, however, to drive Orgeluse from his heart or his dreams. Once more, he must go in search of his love, suffering far more from his love pangs than from the wounds received on the Lit Marveile.

Walk off Ponter's Ball into the ditch and cross the stile at its base. Cross the middle of the field (G) to the stile directly opposite and then continue on the same line until you come to Woodlands Road (H). Turn left and, enjoying the view over the orchard to your left, follow the road until you come to the busy Shepton Mallet road. Cross the A361 with care and turn left. Just after St. Anne's Nursery a post marked 'Norwood Park 1 mile' directs us down an enclosed path. At the end of the path, as we cross the stile into open fields again (I), the other half of Ponter's Ball comes into view. Aim for the far corner of the field, where the path crosses the tip of the earthwork. At the horn's tip cross the stile and the little plank bridge over the rhyne and cross the next field on the same diagonal line in the direction of Norwood Park until you come to the corner of the field.

Gawain's wounds are far from healed and Mistress Love seems likely to drive the wounded knight to his death. Walking about the castle he discovered a pillar, covered in costly gems, revealing the entire country roundabout in its myriad reflections. In these magical images, Gawain sees a knight and a lady riding across the causeway into the meadow:

> "He thought the Pillar had deceived him. But then he saw Orgeluse de Logroys and a courtly knight approaching the quay beside the meadow." [11]

Despite all the beautiful ladies who attend on him, Gawain yearned only for Orgeluse. Reflected in the crystal mirror she appears beside a stream in the form of the universal woman, the moving principle of his life and of life itself. She was now his, and he hers and he was drawn from the service of the things of this world to her, who is not of this world. He has travelled beyond the merely physical — the phallic desire — to a union of both the spirit and the flesh. Both are absorbed in the other and become one. Gawain called for his armour, and, riding out to greet the pair, engaged the knightly companion of Orgeluse in a joust and defeats him. At last, he is re-united with his love. Mocking him still, she says that the greatest challenge of all yet remains. If he succeeds this time, he may sue for her love:

> "You must get me a garland from the twig of a certain tree. If you will give it to me I shall praise your exploit, and then you may ask for my love."

"Madam, wherever that twig may be,' he replied, 'which can win me such high renown and bliss that I may acquaint you with my passion in the hope that you will favour me, I shall cull it unless death prevents me!" [12]

Off they ride in search of the Tree of the Garland.

From the corner of the field the Right of Way continues along the same diagonal line toward Norwood Park. Ploughed fields or crops often make it awkward to continue, however, so we will turn left to join the concrete farm track that will give us easy walking to Wick Lane. This suits our purposes because it will take us along the nose of Maltwood's Capricorn, all the way to its tip at Norwood Park. The line of sight is straightforward in that our direction continues to bend toward the Tor. Rhynes are not dug here as the land is raised above the moor, sloping gently upwards to Avalon's heart. *At the end of the concrete farm track, we arrive at Norwood Park (J).*

Norwood Park has a very attractive stone-built farmhouse with mullioned windows and well-laid gardens, surrounded by the usual modern farm buildings. Once a monastic property, parts of the farmhouse date to the fifteenth century. *Wick Lane can be accessed by using the farm gates to either side of the large modern barn to the left of the farmhouse. I could not follow the Right of Way indicated on the current OS Map which goes round the back of the farmhouse.*

Take the lane immediately opposite Norwood Park farmhouse, which will take you past a row of stone cottages. This quiet lane leads to Stone Down and the foot of the Tor. We will be turning right at the first opportunity, however, and following the farm track toward the campsite at Wick Farm. After a couple of hundred paces down this pleasant lane, we come to a five-barred gate and a stile. Immediately thereafter, to the right, are two ancient Oaks, known locally as Gog and Magog.

To reach the tree Gawain had first to cross a raging torrent that plunges through a deep ravine, which took the utmost of his skill and courage to prevent he and his mount from drowning. (The worst we will have to put up with is mud and puddles following heavy rain.) Still suffering from the wounds received on the Lit Marveille, the effort of dragging himself out of the torrent in his heavy armour all but finished Gawain off. Gawain found the tree, cut off the twig, and made a garland. The traditional interpretation is that the twig was mistletoe cut from an oak. What Gawain had performed was the ancient Druidic rite.

Pliny, writing two thousand years ago, described the ceremony:

"The mistletoe, however, is found but rarely on the oak; and when found is gathered with due religious ceremony, if possible on the sixth day of the moon. Having prepared for sacrifice and a banquet beneath the trees, they bring hither two white bulls.... Clad in a white robe, the priest ascends the tree and cuts the mistletoe with a golden sickle." [13]

Gawain has usurped the function of the King of the Wood and claimed the right to be his successor. He, not Gramoflanz, has won the fair Orgeluse.

As Gawain attempted to leave the wood with the garland, King Gramoflanz rode out to meet him. He is unarmed, with a sparrowhawk on his noble fist. He appeared before Gawain as the Green Man:

"The mantle that he wore was of grass-green samite lined with gleaming ermine and cut so that its points on either side brushed the ground." [14]

Gramoflanz explained how he had abducted Orgeluse and had offered her a crown and all his lands. He had kept her for a whole year but failed to win her love. The beautiful Orgeluse had her own reasons for wanting King Gramoflanz brought down. Gramoflanz had killed her husband, Cindegast, a youth she had loved above all others. He was, she said:

"A fount of quality, untouched by any falsity, his youth fecund of excellence. Pressing up from darkness he had unfolded towards the light and thrust his fame so high that it could be reached by none whom baseness had power to weaken..." [15]

Gramoflanz informed Gawain that he will not fight because he considered it beneath him to fight any less number than two knights together. He has vowed that he would not fight a knight in single combat — unless his name is Gawain — for Gawain's father treacherously killed his father. So it is that the sons face each other to re-enact what had taken place between the fathers. The symbolism of death and renewal is transparent.

Gramoflanz challenges Gawain to a duel, conceding to him alone the honour of fighting him in single combat. Sixteen days hence they will meet at the court of King Arthur and there he will exact payment for his garland.

The origins of this story are lost in prehistory. Certainly there are many parallels in the myths of ancient religions. In 'The Golden Bough', Frazer describes one such myth, this time from ancient Greece, which echoes the tale of Orgeluse, Gawain and Gramoflanz. In the myth of Diana's priest at Nemi, he who would become the King of the Wood must slay his predecessor. Diana is the Goddess

Mother of Life, whose sanctuary was a grove about a lake where the object of veneration was an oak, of which the priest, the King of the Wood, was the consort and protector. The plant that was to be plucked was mistletoe. In obtaining the eternal fruit, which turned gold on being plucked, the hero wins the right to slay his predecessor and become consort to the goddess. [1]

The ancients believed that the life of the oak resided in the mistletoe. During the winter months, when the oak died, the green mistletoe preserved the spirit of the oak. Removing the mistletoe symbolically killed the Oak King and made it possible for the reign of the Holly King to begin. Frazer echoes the story of Gawain and Gramoflanz in his discussion of the significance of the cutting of the mistletoe:

"Hence if that tree was the oak, the King of the Wood must have been a personification of the oak spirit. It is, therefore, easy to understand why, before he could be slain, it was necessary to break the Golden Bough. As an oak-spirit, his life or death was in the mistletoe or the oak, and so long as the mistletoe remained intact, he, like Balder, could not die. To slay him, therefore, it was necessary to break the mistletoe...." [16]

These universal symbols of Death and Resurrection, of Winter and Spring, of the slaying of the Old King are inherited through ageless traditions, folk tales and fire festivals. This is the story of the aged Grail King, awaiting the time when the one will come who is worthy to cut him down and rule in his stead.

We can sense in the calmness of King Gramoflanz the acknowledgement of his eventual defeat. He concedes the love of Orgeluse to Gawain. Spring can now return, both for ourselves and for the land in which we walk, for it is only when we have healed our hearts that we can begin to heal the land. The pain that divides us and makes all our relationships incomplete, works inside of us like the poison in the wound borne by Anfortas, the Grail King. Only love can heal the wound — the love that is expressed when we ask of He who suffers — "What ails you?"

Only through unconditional love can we make ourselves ready to attain the Grail. In following that love we must expect to suffer before we are worthy and finally to surrender ourselves to that Holy Other:

"For even as love crowns you so shall he crucify you...
Like sheaves of corn he gathers you unto himself.
He threshes you to make you naked.
He sifts you free from your husks.
He grinds you to whiteness.
He kneads you until you are pliant;
And then he assigns you to his sacred fire, that you may become
sacred bread for God's sacred feast." [17]

Sadly, the noble oak wood from which Gawain stole his garland of mistletoe is no more. Lionel Smithett Lewis believed the two trees that stand today to be the last sorry remnants of a Druid Grove. Felled by a farmer in 1906, the wood was sold to J. Snow and Son, Timber Merchants, who trade in Glastonbury to this day. The real Magog was cut down, and probably the original Gog. When Lewis was writing in 1922, fragments of the great oaks could still be seen but even in his time, only the two oaks we see today remained alive and standing out of several dozen trees. Then as now, they barely seem to cling to life. He claimed that over 2000 season rings were counted in one of the great fallen oaks, making the Druid Grove contemporary with the time of Christ and the coming of Joseph of Arimathea. [18]

Turn back to return the way you have come, following the farm track as far as the junction with Stone Down Lane. Turn right and continue up the lane toward the Tor. Immediately before the lane becomes sunken and overarched with trees there is a footpath to the left, sign-posted for Gypsy Lane. Take this footpath, following the fence line to the left, as it contours gently around Stone Down to Gypsy Lane. Four stiles are crossed in all until a stile and a farm gate give access to Gypsy Lane above Edgarley Farm. The campsite marked on the OS maps, sadly, no longer exists. The owners, Don and Barbara Saunders, after running the site for many years, finally retired. The atmosphere on the site could only be described as unique, with its curious blend of New Age travellers, weekend hippies, boy scouts, and middle-aged Caravan Clubbers. This campsite was my introduction to Glastonbury's special atmosphere and I remain eternally grateful to the Saunders who provided me with some of the happiest days of my life.

Continue along the lane, past the crossroads, until it rejoins the Shepton Mallet road once more. From here, it is a short walk down the hill to Chalice Well gardens and the Abbey Barn.

Gawain came back from his quest in triumph, bearing the wreath that was cut from the tree. He rode with his lady Orgeluse to the Castle of Marvels, where a multitude of ladies and four hundred knights joust in honour of his victory. Gawain, in effect, achieved all that he set out to do and becomes the master of his world. It was a world, however, of vanity and earthly delights. The Grail was slipping from his grasp.

1. Mary Caine, The Glastonbury Zodiac, (privately published, Kingston, Surrey, 1978) P.123

2. Wolfram von Eschenbach, Parzival, written circa 1210, trans A.T. Hatto, (Penguin Books, 1986) P.157

3. ibid., P258

4. ibid., P.259

5. ibid., P.259

6. ibid., P.269

7. ibid., P.271

8. ibid., P.275

9. ibid., P.283

10. ibid., P.286

11. ibid., P.298

12. ibid., P.302

13. Pliny, Natural History, XVI, 249. Quoted in The Druids, T.D.Kendrick, (first pub. 1927. This ed., Senate, Random House UK, 1996) P.89

14. Wolfram von Eschenbach, P.304

15. ibid., P.308

16. J.G.Frazer, Balder the Beautiful, Vol. 2, (Macmillan and Co. 1913) P285

17. Kahil Gibran, The Prophet, (first pub., 1926. Pan Books 1991), P.13

18. Revd. Lionel Smithett Lewis, Vicar of Glastonbury, Glastonbury, the Mother of Saints, (St. Stephen's Press, Bristol, 1925) P.30

The Sixth Quest

The Mendips and the Footsteps of Jesus

Perceval and the Hermit

VERLOOKING the northern edges of the Vales of Avalon are the Mendips. These hills contain caves and plunging gorges that have provided shelter to two thousand generations of humanity. Sacred circles created by our Neolithic forbears are still visible when the rising sun casts long shadows across fields near Priddy, and alignments of barrows mark the sacred earth in which our Bronze Age forbears laid their warrior dead. Each generation had the same needs as you or I and asked the same questions: "Who am I; where am I going?" Each in their time yearned for the Eternal Grail. We too must search these hills before our hearts are stilled forever and the oak root feeds in the space where we once loved and yearned.

Cheddar Gorge is the best known attraction in the Mendips, where accretions of vulgar souvenir shops, selling cheese and scrumpy, scar its indescribable beauty. Greed dictates that the motor car has unlimited access to the gorge. Poseurs in four-wheel drive vehicles and boy racers compete to endanger the walker and fill the air with a poisonous haze. Cars cannot reach Ebbor Gorge, where we shall walk, and though laughter and conversation will ring about the limestone crags in summer, the obscenity of the internal combustion engine has never penetrated here. For me, Ebbor Gorge is the abode of Merlin — it is a faerie glen, and on misty summer mornings has no match for magic. In mid-winter it can be dank and oppressive, with the mist clinging sullenly to the trees and dripping off the cold limestone crags. Always it touches deeply and it will visit you in the imagination when the memory of lesser places has long since faded.

Much is said of the coming of Joseph of Arimathea to these hills. Legend says he brought the boy Jesus with him when he came to these islands to trade for tin. Joseph of Arimathea is the first of the Grail Kings and the founder of the Eternal Dynasty whose role it is to guard the Precious Vessel. Here in the Mendips is the source of the Golden Legend that inspired the mystic, William Blake, to ask if the feet of Jesus did indeed 'walk upon England's mountains green.'

And from the Mendips Blake gazed across the Vales of Avalon to that New Jerusalem, nestling amidst its sacred hills...

I have to say that the evidence for the presence of Jesus is tenuous. Lionel Smithett Lewis, author of 'St. Joseph of Arimathea at Glastonbury' can quote early Medieval sources for Joseph's presence in Glastonbury, but is struggling to find anything substantial when with regard to the Mendip traditions. Mrs Weeks, postmistress of Priddy in the 1930s, seems to be his oldest source for the legend that Jesus walked these hills. She apparently stated that:

"Mark Simmons who died aged about 90 in 1933, and used to teach in Sunday School and Chapel, would suddenly say to his hearers, "Suppose you saw Jesus coming up the hill again now.""

She also said that Mrs Barker, widow of a former Vicar, "often referred to His coming." [1]

Such is the stuff of legend! We need not concern ourselves too much with the evidence. The association with the Sangreal is an association of the heart and our yearning alone commands its presence. Here walked the Child Jesus and in His Holy Blood Perceval must bathe in order to be worthy of the Grail.

Perceval left the court of Arthur disgraced. In his spiritual anguish, he renounced God and the companionship of the Table Round. From that day, he wandered through forest and wasteland, accomplishing many great deeds, but coming no closer to his heart's desire. After five long years he is no nearer the Grail than when the accusations of Cundrie, the boar-faced woman, drove him from Camelot. The light of the Grail shone dimly and the years in the wilderness did not humble him or bring him closer to his true self. If anything, the five years of wandering hardened his heart.

It is Good Friday. Perceval does not know this — nor, perhaps, does he care. Clad in glittering armour, he rides proudly through the forest, whilst others walk barefoot and penitent on this cold spring morning. He chanced upon a noble family who have put aside their finery in repentance for their sins and in sorrow for the suffering of Jesus. Their calls for him to heed the sorrows of the day stirred his conscience. In following their footsteps to the hermit's cave, he will come face to face with his true self.

Our walk will take us from Wookey Hole, where some say Arthur slew a witch, through Ebbor Gorge to Priddy. Straightforward paths define the route throughout and this is a fine walk whatever the time of year.

The Mendips — Perceval and the Hermit

Two starting points for this walk are offered. Make your choice depending on your mode of transport and the time of year. If you are using public transport, the centre of Wookey Hole is the ideal place to begin the walk. An hourly bus service runs from Wells to Wookey Hole and information can be obtained from the bus station in Wells and from Glastonbury Tourist Information. If travelling by car, parking can be difficult in high season. Wookey Hole has a substantial car park for the Paper Mill and the Caves. It is, however, a private car park and unless you intend to visit the Caves, the owners rather ungraciously threaten to tow your vehicle away. The ideal solution is to combine your walk with a trip to the Caves. Out of season, there is limited on street parking next to the parish church of St. Mary Magdalene. If you are driving it is recommended that you carry on through the village and take the Priddy road. A walker's car park can be found on the right about a mile beyond Wookey Hole. A second walker's car park is available a little further on, which offers spectacular views of Avalon as well as picnic facilities.

Starting at Wookey Hole. An NB before you begin your walk! You may find the directions for the sections of our walk that pass through Ebbor Wood and Gorge a bit confusing. Our return route also passes through the Wood to add to the problem. Given the proximity of the various turns and twists it has not been possible to show all the detail on the map. You are unlikely to get lost, however. The paths and stiles are well made and sign-posted and you should be able to correct any errors without going too far wrong. Remember to read the waymark posts as you leave the wood to check that all is well.

Before beginning the walk take note of the wooded hill that dominates Wookey Hole to the left as we look back down the road to Wells. This is Arthur's Point, where Bronze Age weapons were found, and probably served as a lookout defending the rich settlements of the Mendips from raiders to the south.

With the Caves car park on your left and the church of Mary Magdalene to the right, walk toward the Paper Mill. The road curves to the left, taking us past the Caves entrance. H.E. Balch, in his book on Wookey Hole, suggest that one of the great Celtic tales, that of Kulhwch and Olwen, was set in these caves:

> "Now Arthur comes into the story, he being on his way back to Wales from Devon and Cornwall, where he has been assisting in the task of hunting a great boar. He asks Kulhwch how fares it with his tasks and is told that all are done save one. It has been demanded of him that he should bring the blood of the black witch, the daughter of the white witch, who lived in the cave at the headwaters of the Stream of Sorrow, on the confines of Hell. Two of Kulhwch's men, he was told, had attempted the task, had gone to the cave and found the witch. By her arts, however, she had overcome them and driven them out of the cave. So Arthur himself said he would undertake it. With Carnwennan, his dagger, Arthur slew the Witch and cut her into two parts. And Kaw, of North Britain took the blood of the Witch and kept it." [2]

We continue past Titlands Lane and follow the road, which is signposted for Easton and Cheddar. This is a pleasant lane, quiet except for the height of the tourist season. Traffic can come down toward Wookey at speed, however, so make use of the stretches of narrow pavement to the right of the lane. Continue up the lane until the last house on the right (A), which is a pebble-dashed bungalow,

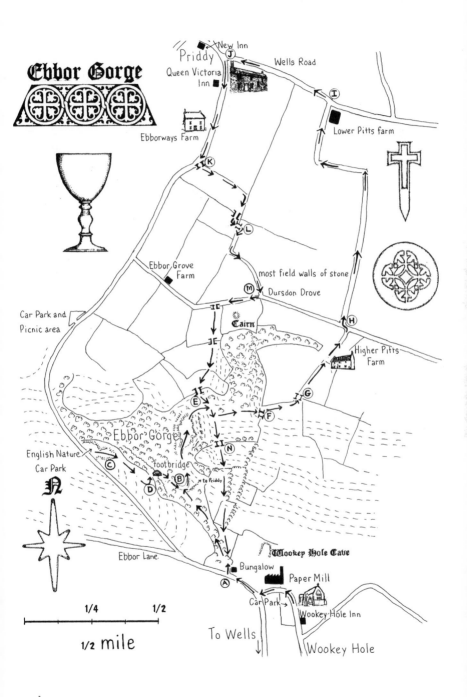

Ebbor Gorge

Priddy
New Inn
Queen Victoria Inn
Wells Road
Ⓙ
Ⓘ
Lower Pitts farm
Ebborways Farm
Ⓚ
Ⓛ
Ebbor Grove Farm
most field walls of stone
Ⓜ Dursdon Drove
Car Park and Picnic area
Cairn
Ⓗ
Higher Pitts Farm
Ⓔ
Ⓖ
Ⓕ
Ebbor Gorge
English Nature Car Park
Ⓒ
footbridge
Ⓝ
Ⓓ
Ⓑ
to Priddy
Ebbor Lane
Wookey Hole Cave
Bungalow
Paper Mill
Ⓐ
Car Park
Wookey Hole Inn
To Wells
Wookey Hole

1/4   1/2

1/2 mile

painted a pale magnolia at the time of writing. Where the pavement ends and immediately after the bungalow turn right to join a path signposted 'Priddy 3 miles'. Follow the path for about thirty metres, where it splits into two. Take the lower path to the left. This is a beautiful, calm green track that slowly merges into a pretty, wooded valley through which a lazy stream flows. In wet weather, the going can be muddy, as horses are regularly exercised here and the clay soil can be very disturbed. The path takes us with a steady, gentle ascent into Ebbor Wood and toward the Gorge. In these lower reaches, the trees are mainly young oaks of perhaps a century or so in age. *At the end of the green track, a five-barred gate marks the entrance to Ebbor Gorge, now in the care of English Nature. Cross the stile and follow the path into the gorge.*

From the gate the path into the gorge is well maintained and is dry and pleasant underfoot regardless of weather or the time of year. As we walk on the sides of the gorge rise higher above us, creating an enclosed and sometimes gloomy world. Always, though, it is a wild and beautiful place and the presence of others does not seem to destroy the sense of peace and privacy.

*After a few hundred metres, the path splits in to three **(B)**. The first path we encounter to our right is waymarked 'Priddy 2½ miles' and ascends a flight of steps. The path to the left beyond this is signposted for the car park. We ignore these and take the second right-hand path into the Gorge.*

Starting at the walker's car-park

*The steep, winding road from Wookey to Priddy follows a spur out of the valley in which Wookey Hole nestles. As you drive out of Wookey and shortly after Titlands Lane on the left, the road forks. Take the right-hand road for Priddy, which rises steeply upwards. Keep your eyes open for an English Nature maintained car park on the right, approximately 500 metres after the junction with the Easton road **(C)**.*

Walk to the back of the car park, where the track loops around two trees. Walk into the loop and pick up the footpath to the gorge to the left of the bench. From here, the path descends gently, running parallel with the road you have just ascended. We pass a stone plinth overlooking the gorge to our left, surmounted with a bronze plaque. The monument informs us that Mrs. G.W. Hodgkinson gave the Gorge and Woodland to the Nation in memory of Sir Winston

Churchill. Mrs Hodgkinson and her husband were also responsible for the work done back in th 1920s to make Wookey Hole Caves accessible to the public. It is worth pausing by the monument as the spot offers inspiring views over the gorge. When mist or low cloud hangs over the vista, we truly seem to gaze into a Grail landscape of mysterious caves and forests where the Questing Beast may lurk.

Follow the path as it continues to descend, with the wooded slopes of the Gorge on our left and the road to our right. The path curves down into the wood, with the steeper sections stepped to make the going easier. At the bottom of the steps, we encounter a track with an old dry-stone wall on the far side. Here we turn left to approach the gorge **(D)**.

We cross a stile by a five-barred gate and follow the path as it descends into the gorge. A fine canopy of trees, their trunks thickly covered with ivy, frame the sky above.

About thirty metres after the gate the path to the gorge forks to the right and is clearly waymarked with an English Nature sign.

The path curves down to a plank bridge over a stream and changes direction to follow the stream toward the Gorge. At the end of the path, where it forks to the left and right, turn left to enter the gorge **(B)**.

Crags of carboniferous limestone appear on both sides as we move deeper into the gorge. Following a route that would once have been a powerful river flowing through dank caves, the path ascends steeply into the narrowing gorge and we enter a strange and mysterious place where the Underworld seems very near. *After a short ascent, the path levels off.* We find ourselves hemmed in by slabs of damp, ivy-covered rock. Above us, the sheer rocky crags, with their crown of overhanging trees add to our sense of claustrophobia.

One cold morning Perceval was riding through such a forest — the endless forest that features so often in Grail Myth that represents the darkness through which we all stumble blindly — when he came across a group of pilgrims:

"A light mantle of snow lay on the ground, yet of a depth that would make us shiver today. This was in a great forest. And now an old knight came towards him, beside whose grizzled beard his skin shone clear. His wife was as grey-haired as he. Over their bare bodies, they both wore coarse grey cloaks on their pilgrimage to and from Confession. Perceval, noble warrior, had cared for his person so well that his magnificent caparison was in all ways worthy of a knight. In such splendid armour did he ride that the clothes of the grey man riding towards him were quite outshone." [3]

The penitents reproached Perceval for riding in such splendour. Did he not realise what day it was? Perceval replied that he had ignored the passing days and years:

"I used to serve one named 'God', till it pleased Him to ordain such vile shame for me."

The grey-haired penitent told him that it is Good Friday, the day that the Son of God gave his life in order to pay our debt of sin and redeem Mankind from Hell. The old man advised him to seek the council of a hermit who lived close by. Perceval spurred his horse on, giving it rein, and for the first time in five years puts himself in God's hands to guide his horse where He will:

"If God's power is so great that it can guide horses and other beasts and people, too, then I will praise His power.... Now go where God chooses!" [4]

The horse took Perceval to Fontane la Salvaesche, where a holy man, named Treverizent, lived his life of prayer and abstinence. From Treverizent, Perceval will learn things about the Grail that have remained hidden. It is at this point in his tale that Wolfram reveals to his readers that, through the maternal line, Perceval is descended from the Grail Kings:

"Titurel and his son Frimutel bequeathed the Grail to Anfortas, whose sister was Herzeloyde on whom Gamuret begot a son to whom this tale belongs." [5]

Perceval was moved that God has heard his prayer and guided his warhorse to Treverizent. For the first time, he is touched with humility and sorrow for his pride. His soul is revealed to him, opening the way for repentence and the Way of the Grail:

"Sir, guide me now: I am a sinner."

We will follow the footsteps of the hermit through the gorge as it narrows further and the limestone crags close in as if to crush us.

Water once crashed about this narrow space, rushing between stalagmites and stalagtites in an icy darkness. Today, the water runs deep beneath us and we must imagine the fast-flowing stream along which Perceval was led.

The hermit led Perceval to a waterfall — le Fontane de Salvaesche — and they passed through the veil of water to a grotto where a charcoal fire burned. Perceval removed his armour, the symbol of his assumed identity, and rested upon a bed of ferns. He discovered in his conversation with the old man how long it was that he had wandered in search of the Grail. Five years had passed since he left the court of Arthur in disgrace, five long years of aimless wandering, achieving fame perhaps, but of the Grail and his heart's desire, nothing.

"Only now do I realise how long I have been wandering with no sense of direction and unsustained by any happy feelings. Happiness for me is but a dream: I bear a heavy burden of grief.... All I sought was battle. I am deeply resentful of God, since he stands godfather to my troubles: He has lifted them up too high, while my happiness is buried alive." [6]

We too have wandered the wild forests and wastelands of our lives, not daring to let go of the routines, the careers, the prejudices and empty relationships through which we blindly wander. Happiness remains utterly elusive. Everything must be shed — all the masks — so that we can see clearly what really matters. We must accept the penance of acknowledging that we are lost. As we walk on, the gorge narrows still further, as if to crush the space in which we walk. Ahead of us, where we can now reach out and touch the opposing walls of the gorge, a flight of ragged rock steps offers an escape. As we climb and the limestone walls close in still further, we are left with the narrowest of clefts through which to escape. Let this be the moment that you summon all the masks that you have worn. See them as your barrier to the Grail. Embodied by your fragmented soul, they block your escape. Now is the time to fight, to tear down the veil, and appropriate what is yours — your true self.

Before you leave the gorge look back and experience the mystery of this otherworld one last time. Despite its beauty, the rocky defiles can create a feeling of oppression, particularly on damp, misty days. As we climb from the Underworld to the open spaces above, we experience the exhilaration that open prospects give after a time of confinement.

It is also the sense of release experienced by the penitent who has unburdened his soul. We pass through the Fountain of Salvation once more.

For five years Perceval searched in vain for the Grail, turning deeper and deeper into himself, yet failing to find the light inside. We too must turn away from the darkness and renew ourselves, dying to the old life and being born again to the new.

Follow the path out of the gorge. At the path junction (E), we turn right for a short distance, and climb to the crest of the ridge above the gorge. Here we find a way-mark for the car park. At the waymark, we turn left (confusion is possible at this point, so if you have a compass check you are walking in an easterly direction). Follow the slope uphill to a stile and five-barred gate way-marked as the West Mendip Way to Priddy (F). (If it says something different walk back to (E) and try again!)

The path takes us from the wooded slopes of the nature reserve to the open, exposed space of the heath, where the autumn winds blows cold and sharp. *A wire fence to our left guides us toward Higher Pitts Farm. Where the fence starts to curve to the left, we come to two gates. Go through the second metal five-barred gate, where there is a way-mark post marked 'Priddy 2 miles' (G). After the gate, follow the hedge-line to the left until you come to Higher Pitts Farm. Take care to follow the arrows that direct you between the farm buildings and don't worry too much about the barking sheep dogs. Always be calm and courteous with dogs doing their duty!*

At the top of the lane past the farm, the track joins Dursdon Drove (H). Here, we turn left and shortly thereafter turn right, cross the cattle-grid, and follow the well-made track to Lower Pitts Farm.

On cold, blustery days, I am grateful for the rapid pace this track affords to the hostelries at Priddy. It may be a good 1¼ mile to Priddy but it is easily attainable in twenty-five minutes at a brisk pace. Beyond the ancient, mossy dry-stone walls that bound the track lie the exposed pastures of the Mendips. In the Vales of Avalon corn and the grapevine flourish and often, when cloud lies heavy on the Mendips, that distant orchard paradise basks in sunshine.

I like to think of Joseph of Arimathea striding purposefully along this ancient track, thorn staff in hand, to Priddy, with the boy Jesus running to keep up. The thought brings a touch of poignancy for the legend goes on to say that, not so many years later, Joseph would return — this time bearing the blood of the crucified child. For some, of course, the precious cruets of blood and sweat are the Sang Real, the true Grail, the Blood of Jesus, shed for the forgiveness of sins and the salvation of the world. As a child attending a Roman Catholic primary school, I remember being told that the shedding of one drop of blood by the Son of God was enough to pay the price for the sins of a thousand worlds. Powerful words from a long-dead teacher called Miss Dilworth that have stuck in my head for four decades now. For the Christians of a thousand years this Grail came to Glastonbury and sanctified the earth on which you walk.

Unlike Peer Gynt, who goes to his grave none the wiser about his true self, Perceval had a turning point, a catharsis that led him back to the foot of the Cross. The hermit told Perceval the story of how God created Adam and how Adam was brought down through Eve's temptation and the work of Lucifer. God himself was to take on Adam's nature of flesh and blood so that the harm done by that first Adam might be undone. He offered Perceval the sacrament of confession so that, after five years in the wilderness, he might make his peace with God.

Perceval confessed that he yearned for his wife and for the Grail. Treverizent replied that to yearn for the Grail is sinful for no man may gain the Grail by his own efforts. Such things are decided in heaven:

> "For no man can win the Gral other than the one who is acknowledged in heaven as destined for it. This much I have to say about the Gral, for I know it and have seen it with my own eyes." [7]

The old man went on to explain how the Grail is guarded by the Templars, who draw their nourishment from the Grail itself:

> "They live from a Stone whose essence is most pure. It is called Lapis exillis. By virtue of this Stone, the Phoenix is burnt to ashes, in which he is reborn.... However ill a mortal may be, from the day on which he sees the Stone he cannot die for that week. For if anyone, maid or man, were to look at the Gral for two hundred years, you would have to admit that his colour was as fresh as in his prime. Such powers does the Stone confer on mortal men that their flesh and bones are soon made young again. This Stone is also called the Gral." [8]

"Today a message alights upon the Gral governing its higher

virtue, for today is Good Friday, when one can infallibly see a dove wing its way down from heaven. It brings a small white Wafer to the Stone and leaves it there." [9]

*Just past Lower Pitts Farm the farm track joins the Wells Road (**I**). We turn left here to follow the road into Priddy. This is rarely a busy road but caution needs to be exercised, particularly in poor visibility.*

*As we arrive at the village (**J**), our route takes us left, following the direction given by a sign to 'The Queen Victoria Inn'.* The equally excellent 'New Inn' overlooks the village green to the right, and that direction will eventually bring us to the Post Office and the village church, with its scattering of Bronze Age Tumuli close by. It is strongly recommended that you take your ease for an hour or two before continuing the Quest. *Once refreshed, our route takes us from the 'Queen Victoria' to the edge of the village at Ebborways farm. About two hundred metres past the farm on the left-hand side of the lane, a way-mark post for Wookey Hole marks the point where we leave the road (**K**).* Take care here as the gentle curve of the lane prevents motorists seeing you from a distance.

Cross the stile and follow the stone wall to the left of the field.

Perceval begged to become one of that Company of knights guarding the Grail, whose names were inscribed by heaven on the top edge of the Stone. Though a sinner, he had sacrificed everything to the demands of chivalry in the hope that he would be found worthy:

"I fought wherever fighting was to be had, so that my warlike hand has glory within its grasp. If God is any judge of fighting He will appoint me to that place so that the Company there know me as a knight that will never shun battle." [10]

Perceval's arrogance is still apparent. There is no purpose behind his violence other than to demonstrate his superiority in arms. In five years, he has learned nothing. Without humility, he can come no closer to the Grail. Perceval's host warns him accordingly:

"There, of all places, you have to guard against arrogance by cultivating meekness of spirit. You could be misled by youthfulness into breaches of self-control. — Pride comes before a fall!" [11]

Pride brought about the fall of Anfortas, the Grail King. The dreadful wound, which caused him so much suffering, was a consequence of hubris. He pursued wealth, fame, and love beyond the bounds of decency and paid the price when he fought Gramoflanz, the King of the Wood, for love of Orgeluse.

Treverizent then said there was a young knight who Providence had called to the service of the Grail but who had been found wanting. The youth had left the Grail Castle carrying a great burden of sin, for he had failed to inquire about his host's hurt. When faced with the sight of Anfortas' dreadful wound, the bleeding lance, even the Gral itself, the young knight had remained silent.

Perceval realised that he was the youth of the tale. Treverizent explained how much suffering the failure to ask the question caused. The young knight had been their last hope. Every remedy that was known had been applied to Anfortas' wound without success:

"There is a bird called Pelican. When it has young it loves them to excess. Instinctive love impels it to pick through its own breast and let the blood flow into its chick's mouths. This done, it dies. We obtained some blood of this bird to see if its love would be efficacious, and anointed the wound to the best of our ability: but it helped us not at all...."

" 'Nephew,' said his host, 'never before or since has the King been in such pain as when the planet Saturn thus announced its advent, for it is its nature to bring great frost. Laying the lance on the wound as had been done before failed to help us, so this time it was thrust into the wound. Whilst the King's frost was being warded off in this way his people were in the depths of despair." [12]

In time it was revealed that their only hope lay in the knight who would come and ask the Question — the noblest and best knight of his age, who by his lineage was destined to become the next Grail King. But the question was not asked and the young knight had ridden away leaving the court of the Grail King in despair of God's mercy.

An overwhelming sense of guilt forced Perceval to confess — that he was the young knight who had come to Anfortas and failed to ask the question:

"The man who rode to Munsalvaesche and saw all the marks of suffering and who nevertheless asked no Question was I, unhappy wretch! Such is my error, my lord." [13]

At the far corner of the field we turn right at the water trough and continue to follow the field boundary. About fifty metres after the trough, the right of way crosses to the other side of the wall via a traditional stone slab stile (L). A Wookey Hole waymark confirms your route. Thereafter a wall and a fence enclose the right of way. This confined path can be a bit squelchy and slippery underfoot in wet weather.

The enclosed path takes us back to Dursdon Drove, where we turn right (M). We follow the drove down a gentle decline until a hollow is reached with a small pond to the right. The path then rises out of the hollow and to your left, you will see a stile. Cross the stile and follow the left-hand field boundary. Take note of the ancient cairn and probable burial mound in the field to the left. The path runs to the right of the depression that descends into Ebbor Wood and this will bring you to a stile at the right hand tip of the wood. This is another fine traditional stone slab stile. Cross the next field along the same line, locating the stile in the crumbling dry-stone wall on the other side of the field. Continue on the same line of approach until you come to a stile giving access to Ebbor Wood. Cross the stile and descend the slope into the wood, keeping to the clearly defined path. From the bottom of this path (E), the way back to the walker's car park is waymarked. If you parked at the English Nature Car Park follow the waymarks back to the car park.

Having established Perceval's identity, the hermit revealed that he is his uncle, the brother of Herzeloyde, his mother. The story of Perceval's family and circumstances are revealed by the old man and for the first time Perceval discovered the truth about his family and ancestry. In effect, he is given the identity he never had. He discovered that the Red Knight, Ither by name, whom he had slain so eagerly and looted of his armour, was also related to him. Perceval had slain his own flesh and blood. Further, in stripping the knight of his horse and armour he had broken the most basic rules of chivalry. Even greater misfortune was revealed to Perceval. When he had ridden off to pursue his glory, his mother, Herzeloyde, collapsed on the earth in grief for her departed son. She had died shortly after of a broken heart. Her only surviving child had never thought to ask about her well being and did not know of his own mother's passing:

"You were the Beast she suckled, the Dragon that flew away from her.... You are of the same stock as Ither, yet ignoring the ties of blood you raised your hand against him. But God has not forgotten him. If you mean to lead a life of trust towards God, you must atone to Him for this. I tell you in sorrow; for you have two great sins. You slew Ither; and you caused your mother's death. Because of the great love she bore you she did not survive your going away and leaving her. Now do as I advise: do penance for your misdeeds and have a care for your ending, so that your toil here on the earth earns you peace for your soul above." [14]

Thus it was that Trevizerent heard Perceval's confession and took his sins from him. Perceval must now leave to claim his birthright — the crown of the Grail King and the guardianship of the Grail.

"Give me your sins! I shall vouch for your penitence before God. And do as I have instructed you: let nothing daunt you in this endeavour.... They took their leave of one another. Elaborate how, if you wish." [15]

*The way back to Wookey is straight ahead at **(E)**, ascending to the crest of the hill and then down to the edge of the wood, where a stile and five-barred gate provide an exit from the nature reserve **(N)**. From the gate, a pleasant path takes us gently across the field to a gap in the tree line. Fine views of Wookey and Wells beyond provide a direction to aim for. This pleasant green path across rolling fields descends graciously toward Wookey Hole and we need do no more than keep to the same direction. In time, the bungalow that marked the start of our walk comes in to view. Again, we negotiate the ground torn by the hooves of exercising horses at the bottom of the hill before following the path to the road **(A)**. A left turn past the bungalow will bring us back to the paper mill and the centre of Wookey Hole.*

In his confession, Perceval must peel the many-layered onion, just as Peer Gynt did. Each layer is a mask that he has worn for want of an identity that he can call his own. Each sin is a consequence of assuming the values of the world seen through a mask. Now he must take off the masks one by one.

Instead of finding a void when the last mask is taken away what Perceval confronts is God. God seeing him — he seeing himself reflected in God's eyes. It is recognizing what he knew all along but had somehow lost — that we are one with Creation and one with the Creator who manifests Himself in the Presence of Creation. The ecstatic vision of the mystic is not the Vision of God. What the mystic experiences is God seeing Himself. When all the masks are stripped away, the eyes that see are the eyes of God.

"Beyond this there is often a numinous experience of this inner psychic wholeness. This experience is usually accompanied by a profound emotion which the ego senses as an epiphany of the divine. For this reason it is practically impossible to differentiate between an experience of God and an experience of the Self." [16]

The idea of redemption through self-knowledge is not new. It lies at the heart of the confessional and if we do not seek forgiveness in self-knowledge then we ask forgiveness for a stranger. Like Lear, Perceval is a man who has "but slenderly known himself." He too must find himself before he can be healed and become worthy of the Grail once more.

And the redemption that we seek is for the sin of Eden, the sin of Pride that first separated Man from the Divine. Pride drove Lucifer out of Paradise because he separated himself from God. From his crown fell the stone that became the Gral of Wolfram's Parzival. The sin of pride lies precisely in our claim to be separate — to being alone. Only when we are stripped of all our masks will pride fall away. When we are naked, we can better acknowledge our relationship with the Divine. Then we shall know the way back.

Only then may we embark on what Plotinus described as "The flight of the alone to the Alone."

1. Revd. Lionel Smithett Lewis, Vicar of Glastonbury, Glastonbury, the Mother of Saints, (St. Stephen's Press, Bristol, 1925) P.162

2. H.E.Balch, The Great Cave of Wookey Hole, (The Cathedral Press, Wells, 1932) P.73

3. Wolfram von Eschenbach, Parzival, written circa 1210, trans A.T. Hatto, (Penguin Books, 1986) P.229

4. ibid., P.231

5. ibid., P.233

6. ibid., P.235

7. ibid., P.239

8. ibid., P.239

9. ibid., P.240

10. ibid., P.241

11. ibid., P.241

12. ibid., P.250

13. ibid., P.248

14. ibid., P.253

15. Wolfram Von Escenbach, P255

16. Emma Jung & Marie-Louise von Franz, The Grail Legend, trans. Andrea Dykes, (Sigo Press, Boston 1986) P.99

The Last Quest

The Attainment of the Grail

Glastonbury Tor

LASTONBURY Tor is a place where fact and fantasy collide and have done so for thousands of years. It is a gateway where all worlds meet and within its grassy slopes lie more mysteries than are contained within the Great Pyramid. St. Michael's Tower crowns the summit, pointing like a giant finger to the heavens, and beneath its cracked foundations, are labyrinths leading to the underworld. It is a conspiracy of space and time. Formed in the depths of the sea and thrust up over countless aeons, it measures time slowly. Humans came late to this hill and made it a place of dreaming, expressing through the work of their hands the feeling within, the yearning for

that which we cannot quite articulate. They catch us unawares —
those brief intuitions from our unconscious — and we must hang on
to them for they are glimpses of the Grail.

Katherine Maltwood described the Tor as Aquarius, the Water
Bearer, with Chalice Well forming the Urn of Aquarius. The Tor has
many springs and yields vast amounts of water throughout the year.
It is, indeed, the Water Bearer. Aquarius also symbolises the Grail,
the sacred vessal from which pours the fulfillment of all our hopes
and dreams. It is the heart of the Grail Quest. It is Munsalvaesche,
the Mount of Salvation, on which was built the Temple of the Grail.

Between 1964 and 1966 the Chalice Well Trust commissioned three
seasons of excavations on the summit of the Tor. Substantial
evidence was uncovered for an Arthurian settlement, although the
construction of the medieval church destroyed much of the
archaeology from this period of occupation. It was on the slopes that
sherds of Mediterranean amphorae were found, linking the
community on the Tor with the same trading network that brought

similar goods to Cadbury Camelot and Tintagel Castle in Cornwall. Thus the three places that folklore links most intimately with Arthur knew the presence of a powerful warlord during the Arthurian period.

Philip Rahtz, who carried out the excavations, points out that tradition and legend link the Tor with a character from Arthurian legend, a warlord called Melwas. He was responsible for the abduction of Guinevere, and Arthur besieged him here. But the Tor's defenses proved too strong and peace had to be mediated by Gildas, then a monk of the abbey, in order to effect Guinevere's release. [1]

Some believe that the monastery on the Tor was the first in Britain and was a focus of pilgrimage from the earliest days of Christianity. The popularity of the hilltop monastery as a place of pilgrimage was such that the monks could not cope with the number of pilgrims. As a consequence, the main body of the community moved to lower ground. Thus, the Tor was the place where Glastonbury's monastic community began, and where it was finally destroyed. The last abbot, Abbot Whiting, with two monks, Robert Jacob and John Thorn, were hanged, drawn and quartered on its summit by Henry VIII's servants, following the dissolution of the monastery.

The Tor remains a focus for pilgrimage, both mainstream and esoteric. Druids and witches celebrate the passing seasons on the Tor. Whirling Dervishes see their mystic practices reflected in the spiralling terraces and Hindu, Buddhist and Ba'hai have worshipped in the shadow of St. Michael's Tower. It can be a gathering place for the local community on special occasions. On the morning of the last solar eclipse thousands of sky-gazers squeezed on its tiny summit, as if the Second Coming was imminent. Roman Catholics and devotees of the Goddess complete their pilgrimages here, as do more religious groups than I would care to name. It seems inconceivable that the Tor's spiritual role belongs only to the Christian era. I have no doubt that this was a sacred place when the Sweet Track was built by our Stone Age forbears, who fished and hunted in the marshes at the foot of this sacred island six thousand years ago.

So it is to the Tor that we come as seekers of the Grail, as indeed many have come before, searching for a buried cup or an entrance to another world. Only we know better. The treasure we seek is a healing of the Self and the vision of the Grail within:

"In the centre of the Castle of the Grail, our own body, there is a shrine, and within it is to be found the Grail of the heart. We should indeed seek to know and understand that inhabitant. It is the fragment of the divine contained within each one of us — like the sparks of unfallen creation which the Gnostics saw entrapped within the flesh of the human envelope. This light shines within each one, and the true quest of the Grail consists in bringing that light to the surface, nourishing and feeding it until its radiance suffuses the world." [2]

An accident of nature and history has given us Glastonbury Tor. On its summit is a hollow tower and through its unroofed space we may watch the wheeling vault of the heavens. Watch closely and you will see shooting stars — angels flying from Paradise. One such angel was Lucifer, the Bearer of Light, who Michael cast from Paradise. In its tower, Glastonbury Tor symbolises that eternal tension between Good and Evil, between Self-Knowledge and the Mask. Today the Question will be asked and Satan, the eternal shape-shifter who masks the divine spark in us all, will be cast back into hell once more and forever. Today we will tear off the Mask and behold the Grail.

The Last Quest

Our last walk begins at the top of Glastonbury High Street (A). Facing us at the top of the High Street is a fine old stone-faced building called Summer House, and to the right of it the Victorian Methodist Chapel. Sandwiched between the two is a drinking fountain, no longer functioning, in a curious neo-romanesque style,with red granite columns. This is a suitable reminder of the medieval setting of our Quest and echoes some of the architecture of the Abbey. *Cross the road and carry straight on along the ascending road known as Bove Town.* You will encounter a lime green painted Gospel Hall on the right, which has been here since the nineteenth century.

To the left as you walk up Bove Town is Edmund Hill, now covered by an unsightly housing estate, with modern housing being steadily shoe-horned on to every last scrap of land. Scant regard has been given to aesthetics. To the right of Bove Town modern developments

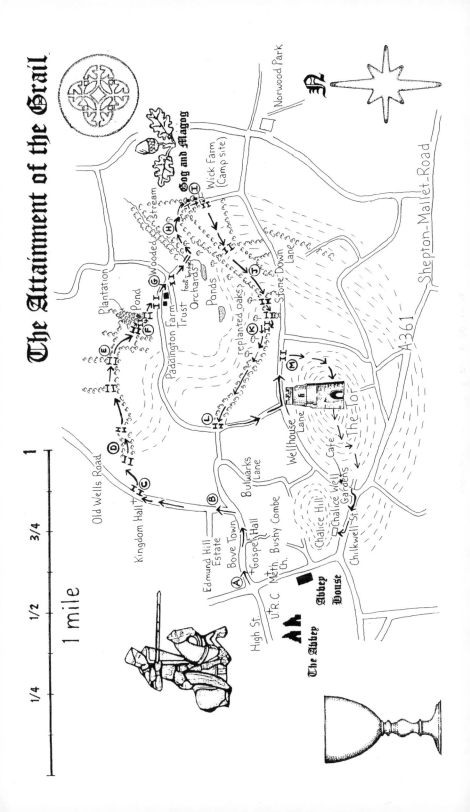

have eaten into Bushy Combe — once one of Glastonbury's little gems. Bove Town itself has retained some of its character and there are a small number of interesting and beautiful houses to be seen along the way. On the left, for example, can be found Jacoby Cottage — converted from a chapel, with its traceried window and remains of a gothic arch in its leaning gable end. This is Glastonbury's only surviving slipper chapel, dating back to the fifteenth century, where pilgrims left their shoes before walking barefoot to St. Michael's church on the Tor. The Victorian houses on the right soon give way to cottages of an earlier provenance. Take note of the big Blue Lias slabs, utilised to form earth retaining walls for the gardens on the right-hand side of the road before and after Bushy Combe Gardens. Some say these are pilferings from the Abbey ruins. It will do well to run your hand over the rough surfaces of these stones and reflect upon the feet of the monks and pilgrims who walked up this same lane several centuries ago. Sadly, their meditative pace is not matched by the traffic on Bove Town today. Local people, mainly from the Edmund Hill estate, roar up and down it at speeds that defy both sanity and safety. In between cars, you will find the songbirds still active, refusing to be displaced by either developers or road traffic.

*At Wick Hollow **(B)** we turn left to follow the Old Wells Road down to the Levels.* At the crest of the hill, we are greeted with a fine view of the Mendips some six miles distant. As we descend the road becomes noticeably quieter and the feel of the walk more rural. To the left we pass a modern Kingdom Hall of Jehovah's Witnesses — a reminder that everyone of a religious bent likes to have a foothold in God's Own Country.

*Immediately after the Kingdom Hall on the right-hand side of the road is a stile **(C)** and a 'public footpath' post. After crossing the stile look down into the valley and you will see a hedged green lane and a five-barred gate, toward which streams flow. Walk down toward the green lane.* At last, open countryside stretches out in front of us and the claustrophobia of urban life is left behind.

Glittering on the verdant field, the sun catches the armour of two knights approaching each other at a gallop from opposite sides of the field. We pause, fascinated and afraid, to watch the outcome of the conflict.

As Perceval crossed an open space between two great forests, he was to meet an adversary who was to prove a match for him. The man was an infidel king, who had come to these shores with a mighty army. In search of adventure he had left his army camped by the seashore. The wealth of this king was unimaginable. The jewels encrusting his armour could not be bought with the wealth of a kingdom. Fate was to bring these two great adversaries together and put the redemption of Anfortas, the Grail King, in jeopardy once more.

The two knights levelled their lances and charged. They clashed with such ferocity that lances shattered into splinters — and yet neither man was unhorsed. When several lances had been broken and the collarbones of both men were in pieces they dismounted to continue their battle with heavy broadswords. The clashing of fine steel rings about our little combe and sunlight flashes from the arching blades, momentarily dazzling us. Surely, such ferocity means that one of them must die.

What neither foe knew, as they continued their death-struggle, was that they shared the same father.

"The Infidel threw his sword high up, a rain of blows forced Perceval to his knees. Whoever wishes to name them 'two' is entitled to say 'Thus did they fight.' Yet, they were no more than one. Any brother of mine and I make one person, as do a good man and his good wife." [3]

Thus it was that the surviving sons of Gahmuret, one born a heathen to Belacane, an African queen, and the other the child of Herzeloyde, are tricked by fate into a fight to the death. They seemed evenly matched, until Perceval struck the heathen a blow on his helmet and broke his sword:

"The stout sword of Gaheviez was shattered by a blow on the Infidel's helmet which brought the bold and mighty stranger to his knees. It was no longer pleasing to God that Perceval should wield a weapon robbed from a corpse, as though this were right and proper: for this was the sword he had taken from Ither, knowing no better in his youthful ignorance." [4]

His magnanimous foe did not take advantage of the broken sword, but immediately offered a truce, acknowledging that he would have been defeated had Perceval's sword not broken. The two sat together on the grass and the infidel volunteered his name. Perceval knew he had a brother who was described to him as having skin that was part black and part white. Feirefiz, lord of Tribalibot, son of Gahmuret, their common father, removed his helmet and coif to reveal himself as the brother that Perceval had never known. Their strife ended with an embrace and a kiss.

Feirefiz was an Arab. At the time that Wolfram was writing, the Saracens were the mortal enemy of Christendom. The combat between Feirefiz and Perceval symbolised the conflict between the flower of two great civilizations. With the illusion of armour removed and the Sword of Pride destroyed, the enemies are revealed to each other as brothers — essentially as one flesh. This is the final step in the perfecting of Perceval, in which all his battles are perceived as a struggle with himself and his own pride and ambition. In their embrace forgiveness and healing encompass the living web of all humanity.

At the bottom of the field is a five-barred gate (D). Cross the stile to the right of the five-barred gate and follow the lane. This pleasant hedged path is known locally as Holywell Lane, and once led, according to tradition, to one of Glastonbury's sacred springs. It offers an abundance of peace to the walker and the town is already forgotten. To our left, across open farmland is an almost uninter-rupted view of Wells and the Cathedral, with its fine restored tower a creamy white in the sun. *At the end of the lane cross the stile (avoiding the mud in wet weather) and follow the hedge-line to the right of the field.* Invisible to us at this time is St. Michael's Tower and our destination at the summit of the Tor.

At the corner of the field cross the plank bridge and the stile and continue to follow the hedge to the right. At the corner of the next field cross the stile (E) and continue following the hedge-line until the narrow field opens out. Cross the field at a diagonal, walking slightly uphill toward a small plantation. Cross the stile in the corner of the field and follow the right-hand fence-line through the plantation (F). At the far side of the plantation cross the stile, walk past the little fenced-off pond to the left and then cross the stile immediately after the pond. On the far side of the field, you will see Higher Wick Farm, now run by Paddington Farm Trust. Cross the field diagonally, aiming for the centre of the farm buildings. As we cross this field, St. Michael's Tower comes into view to our right, rising above Stone Down. *A stile gives us access to a lane that runs round the farm buildings.* There is an ornamental pond opposite, and the fine farm buildings have been attractively restored. Paddington Farm Trust, which runs the farm, is a charitable organisation, which offers rural experiences for children and young people from inner city backgrounds. Keep your eyes open for the varied and interesting livestock on the farm. *Follow the track round the farm to a 'T' junction and then cross the stile directly ahead (G). Follow the wire fence down into the hollow and the wooded stream that runs at the base of Stone Down Hill.*

Cross the new stile and the little footbridge over the stream. In front of us are the lower slopes of Stone Down Hill. Planted on the opposite side of the field is a line of young oaks, protected at the time of writing by frames of wood and wire. Walk across to these and then bear left and walk to where the hedge takes a right hand bend (H). Walk between the line of young oaks and the tree-lined hedge to where the field narrows into a corner and a five-barred gate. The row of young oaks, planted to replace those cut down in 1906, lead to Gog and Magog. The planting of the oaks is part of the outstanding work of the Glastonbury Conservation Society, which has planted thousands of trees in the area. If time and nature are allowed to do their work, and the goodwill of farmers and planners permit, this will be a superb avenue of oaks in two hundred years time. Druids celebrating the Summer Solstice of 2200 will be able to process to the Tor from Gog and Magog entirely protected by their shade. Sadly, the human span is too short for you or I to have that privilege, but we can thank those who have the humanity and foresight to toil for the good of generations yet unborn. Please God, let their work survive, for the developer's greed threatens every precious inch of this sacred land.

Cross the stile next to the five-barred gate to the farm track (I). Immediately to our left are Gog and Magog, the sorry remnant of the grove of ancient oaks, destroyed in 1906. Some give these oaks a Druidic origin, others a Christian. Ancient tradition states that the oldest oak marks the landing place of Joseph of Arimathea and was called the 'Oak of Avalon'. Herne recorded the tradition in 1772, in his 'History and Antiquities of Glastonbury:

> "I was told by the innkeeper, where I set up my horses...that Joseph of Arimathea landed not far from the town, at a place, where there was an oak planted in memory of his landing, called the Oak of Avalon." [5]

We have already visited Gog and Magog. Gawain came here before us, and stole the wreath of mistletoe from the King of the Wood. The ancient oaks will serve as symbols for us once more — this time as the solar and lunar trees of the Grail Kingdom. These two sacred oaks, representing the Sun and the Moon, the masculine and feminine power to renew life, provide a love theme for our walk and a link with the attainment of the Grail.

In Wolfram's tale, Feirefiz will be with his brother in the fulfillment of the Quest at Munsalvaesche, the mountain on which the Grail Castle stands. There, Feirefiz will behold Repanse de Schoye, a maid of unsurpassed beauty. By her alone did the Grail permit itself to be carried:

> "Great purity dwelt in her heart. The flesh without was a blossoming of all brightness." [6]

Feirefiz, whose infidel status prevented him from 'seeing' the Grail — a privilege granted only to those of true faith — fell madly in live with Repanse de Schoye. This son of Gahmuret of Zazamanc was in torment for love of the sister of the Grail King, Anfortas:

"All the longing in my heart is for her... Of all the days since the shield became my shelter, this is my day of deepest affliction." [7]

Feirefiz is told that baptism will not only enable him to behold the Grail but also to sue for the love of Repanse de Schoye, the bearer of the Grail. The following morning, in a font made of ruby and jasper at the heart of the Grail Temple, and before the Grail itself, he was baptised, all for love of the maiden:

"Whatever will assure me of winning that maiden shall be done and seen to be done, fully and faithfully... In the name of your aunt's God, baptise me! "said the infidel as he stood ready for baptism." [8]

Shortly thereafter, amidst much sadness at his going, Feirefiz departed with his bride for the East. Wolfram described how in India she bore a son called John, who was known to medieval Grail mythology as Prester John, a mysterious, all-powerful eastern sovereign, who would come to the aid of Christendom in its hour of need.

In some medieval legends, the kingdom of Prester John is identified with Avalon. In this eastern kingdom there are two trees — that may be described as a Solar and a Lunar tree — which confer universal power on he who beholds the one, and eternal life from the other. The combined balsam from the two trees confer on the king who is anointed with it the power of eternal life so that he may return when his kingdom has need of him. The journey of the mortally wounded Arthur to Avalon is indeed a revisiting of this theme, where, having been healed of his wounds, he becomes 'the Once and Future King.' [9]

This time we will draw the healing energy from these two trees and carry it with us to Munsalvaesche. There we will apply the balm to the wounded king and to our own hearts that we too may be healed.

Perceval and his mottled, half black, half white brother have followed us from the little brook, riding their warhorses to the avenue of young oaks and then dismounting as they approach Gog and Magog. They too, pause to admire the oaks, remembering a tale, already ancient, of the coming to this place of the man who was to be the first of the Grail Kings, bringing with him the Chalice of the Last Supper and the Holy Blood. The man was Joseph of Arimathea, the first Guardian of the Grail and Perceval's ancestor through the maternal line.

A few paces after Gog and Magog we come to a second five-barred gate and stile. Immediately after is a stile in the hedge to the right which takes us into a field that sweeps upwards toward the Tor. Cross the stile into the field. This beautiful path is clearly visible in the grass and is not to be rushed on a hot day.

All about us is a glittering display of colourful pavilions, of squires and pages in the finest livery, and beautiful women accompanied by strumming minstrels. Amidst the pavilions, tables are set out in great rings, where kings, knights and nobles lavishly entertain each other. Mattresses covered in rich silks and brocades are prepared where, having eaten and drunk their fill, the flower of knighthood may relax in the sun and be entertained by the conversation of the most beautiful of noblewomen. Perceval and Feirefiz are welcomed joyously and feted by all. The celebrations carry on into the night, where a thousand torches light the field and the fires crackle about the turning roasts of deer and fowl, fresh-killed by fine hunting dogs and the keen-eyed falcon.

The following day a ring was created in the field to represent the Round Table and all those who were worthy enough to call themselves its Companions met. In great spendour, and surrounded by hundreds of beautiful women, Arthur invited the noble Feirefiz to become a Companion of the Table Round, an honour he happily accepted.

Perceval had quested for the Gral for many a year, and because he was unworthy, he had failed. His repentance has made him worthy once more, and, to acknowledge this, the boar-faced Cundrie appeared again that day at Arthur's court. She addressed Perceval as she had done five years previously — but this time to bring him honour:

> "Now be modest and yet rejoice! The inscription has been read: you are to be Lord of the Gral.... You have won through to peace of soul and outlived cares to have joy of your body." [10]

Perceval shed tears of happiness and asked only how soon he may set out for the Grail Castle. Cundrie told him that his family will share in his joy and he has been granted the further boon of choosing a companion who may join him in the Fellowship of the Grail. Perceval chose his brother, Feirefiz, who agreed to accompany him to Munsalvaesche. After much celebration in which Feirefiz disposed fabulous gifts on every member of Arthur's court, the two brothers armed themselves and set off, guided to Munsalvaesche by Cundrie.

The stile at the top of the field is known locally as 'The Spiral Gate'. It is a special place, however, where I often pause to catch my breath and enjoy the view. On my last visit, the thorn trees to either side of the stile had been bound together with ribbons to create an arch. If you seek a blessing, tie your own scrap of cloth to these trees, preferably from an item that has been a part of your life. Then something of you is left to accrue the blessings of wind and rain and the passing seasons. *Cross the stile at the top of the field and continue upwards toward the brow of the hill (J)*. Soon, Saint Michael's Tower comes into view and the way back to the Grail Castle will be clear. From where we stand, the Tor appears as a conical hill, like an eroded pyramid topped with a tower. The sunlight shining through the entrance arch can be seen from here and the spectacle at sunset can be truly magical. Below, to the right, as we follow the escarpment of Stone Down, is the expansive splendour of the vales of Avalon. Here indeed the land seems poised for the Question that must be asked:

"What ails you?"

And this time the question will be asked and the land healed.

The courtiers of Anfortas, the Grail King, suffer with their lord. Experiencing a pain that is ice and fire, Anfortas pleaded to be allowed to die. But the wounded king must live on and is carried before the Grail that he might not die. The knights and ladies who serve him weep for his pain, but now their sorrow is tinged with hope. The Gral has spoken. In the priceless emerald that is the Gral the words appeared that prophesied Perceval's return. This time he would not fail and the Kingdom of the Grail would pass to him and Anfortas would be released from his pain at last. But that is the future and now he suffers, as his wound suppurates and his followers use herbs to hide the stench of its decay:

"When sharp and bitter anguish inflicted severe discomfort on Anfortas they sweetened the air for him to kill the stench of his wound. On the carpet before him lay spices and aromatic terebinth, musk, and fragrant herbs. To purify the air there were also theriac and costly ambergris: the odour of this was wholesome. Wherever people trod on the carpet, cardamom cloves and nutmeg lay crushed beneath their feet for the sake of the fragrance — as these were pounded by their tread the evil stench was abated." [11]

Cundrie was the escort for the noble brothers and together they rode through forest and wilderness to Munsalvaesche. A company of well-armed Templars set out from the Castle to intercept the three as they approached its gates. When they saw Cundrie they recognised the Turtle Doves — the Arms of the Grail Knights — that adorned her habit. Her return meant that she had been successful in her search for Perceval and their sorrows would soon be at an end:

"Our trouble is over! What we have longed for ever since we were ensnared by sorrow is approaching us under the Sign of the Gral! Rein in! Great happiness is on its way to us!" [12]

Continue to follow the hedge-line to the right. Cross the stile where the field narrows into a point. We cross another stile immediately to our right (K) and we see that we have rejoined the avenue of infant oaks on their progress to the Tor. This green lane is known locally as Paradise Lane. Below us is the dramatic sweep of Stone Down, with ponds and fine orchards nestling in the lee of the hill. The association of the name Paradise with the apple orchards is significant. The apple became a symbol of the Fall, of our loss of Paradise. And yet it is to Avalon — to the Isle of Apples, that Arthur came to be healed of his grievous wound:

"According to Geoffrey of Monmouth, the mortally wounded King Arthur was carried to Insula Avallonis, the Island of Apples.... This apple island is analogous to the Isles of the Blest of antiquity, where golden apples were tended by divine maidens, and to the Celtic "Land of the Living,"likewise situated in the West.... This apple orchard signifies the second Paradise, the goal and salvation that have to be rediscovered after the loss of the first Paradise through the instrumentality of an apple tree." [13]

Ahead of us, the Company of Templars have reached the winding path that leads to the summit of Munsalvaesche and the Grail Temple. *We follow the hedge, now to our left, on this often muddy stretch of path. Sometimes it can be easier to step to the right hand side of the line of young oaks to avoid the quagmire that the cattle can*

166

create in wet weather. In the height of summer it is usually firm and dry and is pleasant level walking. Follow the path until you come to a stile. Cross the stile to join the farm track, which is a continuation of Paradise Lane, and follow it to the metalled road (L). Turn left and follow this fine lane toward the Tor. When you arrive at a 'T' junction with a bench to your right, turn left to follow the road that curves around the base of the Tor. Soon you will come to the entrance to the Tor fields (M), usually apparent from the Ice Cream van parked outside and the sundry vehicles ignoring the parking restrictions.

Slowly, we will walk the path that leads to the summit of the Tor. Ahead of us the Templar knights hold high their pennoned lances in triumph, cheering in unrestrained joy for the coming of he who they have prayed for night and day. Bright are their surcoats of white, emblazoned with the ruddy cross of the Saviour. The very heart of their kingdom had lain prostrate and in pain, darkening the whole land and creating a wasteland. Already the sun has risen, the frost is gone from the wound of Anfortas and from the wounded land. The blossom is seen on the apple tree for the first time in many a year. Their cheers are carried to the glittering battlements of the Grail castle, resounding in the jeweled halls of the Temple and bringing hope to the King who lies within.

With tears of joy, the Company has come to Munsalvaesche, where they are greeted by a multitude of knights, pages, and men-at-arms. Perceval and Feirefiz are brought before the still suffering Anfortas.

Anfortas reminded Perceval of his past failure and that even now he should feel remorse for the suffering he has caused. With his successor come, he pleaded with Perceval to allow him to die, thus ending his unendurable agony:

> "I have suffered torments of expectation, wondering if you were going to restore me to happiness. If you are a man of reputation and honour, ask the knights and maidens here to let me die, and so end my agony. If you are Perceval, keep me from seeing the Gral for seven days and seven nights — then all my sorrows will be over." [14]

Perceval wept. He asked if he might be brought before the Gral to affirm that he indeed was the chosen one. Then he genuflected thrice before the Trinity and turned to his uncle once more. This time, the question was asked:

"Dear Uncle, what ails you?"

Then a miracle took place — for Anfortas was healed of his wound, and his face became radiant with a beauty that surpassed even that of Perceval, for the vision of God had filled his soul. We can only imagine the joy of Anfortas. After years wracked with unendurable and mortal pain and kept alive against his will, the foul and festering wound is healed.

The entire company of Templars immediately acknowledged Perceval as their king. By this Divine act, Perceval proved that his name was writ upon the Gral. No other election was needed.

Now ask the question of yourself. Do not be disturbed by the milling crowds on a busy day. They are here as the representatives of humanity in all its hues. When you are healed, they too will be healed, for we are one, divided only by a different perception. Look out, gaze to the far horizons, and let the question well up within. Ask it of yourself, ask it of these people, ask it of the whole world, stretched out beneath you to the seven seas. Ask it, and listen in that deep inner quiet of your soul for the answer:

"What ails you?"

Our possessions are mere filthy bandages covering the wound that pains us. We are both Perceval and the Fisher King, old and new, youth and age. Beneath the cover of material wealth, possessions, houses, cars, careers, the whole accretion of modern life, lies an injured Self. Pierced through the thighs, impotent, we suffer unendurable pain because we cannot simply be. The wound is Identity, it is the Mask, which is made of iron and binds our soul and heart. Now is the time to be rid of the mask. Ask the question and be healed:

"What ails you?"

The Grail will fill the space that is left. It will manifest itself from within.

"In the centre of the Castle of Brahma, our own body, there is a small shrine, in the form of a lotus flower, and within can be found a small space. We should find who dwells there and want to know him...for the whole universe is in him and he dwells within our heart." [15]

Thereafter, Blancheflor, Perceval's queen and their two young sons, Kardeiz and Loherangrin, were brought to Perceval to take their place as Queen and heirs of the Grail Kingdom. His happiness was complete.

That night preparation was made for the Gral to be brought forth. The Gral was only brought before the Company of the Grail on special occasions. The last time Perceval had beheld the Gral, the Bleeding Lance, the significance of which he had not understood at the time, preceded it. Now the Gral would be carried in to them with jubilation, for their sorrows were over.

The Grail, the horn of plenty — shed its gifts of its abundance to all who served it and gave each one their heart's desire:

"With ceremony they received from the Gral meats both wild and tame: for this man mead, another wine, each according to his custom; mulberry wine, tinctured clary." [16]

In the same way that Wolfram's Gral is a fragment of Paradise, displaced by the vengeful pride of Lucifer, the Grail is the spark that comes from our innermost self, lighting the way back. When we see that light, we will know that you and I are One, that the earth and the sky are One, that the whole sphere of existence is our Spirit and Soul. Then the love of self is turned inside out and becomes the love of the Holy Other. Time will cease, for we are at the beginning and end of all things. Our union with all that is in that first moment of creation will be reflected in our eyes — for all that is was an undifferentiated One in that primordial fire. In the moment of revelation, death is banished from the world, now and for all time.

Tens of thousands climb the Tor each year. Young parents and their eager or unwilling children — Druids, pilgrims, Mother Goddess seekers, latter-day hippies, the green wellie brigade, Japanese, Dutch, Germans, Americans looking for Arthur's burial place — indeed the whole world and its dog come to the Tor on a bright summer afternoon. Not that I mind; part of the interest of the Tor lies in people watching. I have to express a preference, however, for those times when a convocation of didgeridoos and African drums reverberate through the air in the early evening, to the heady smell of ganja and incense. I am old enough to enjoy the bright colours of hippy folk and travellers, with their love of dread-locks and beads that are so reminiscent of a lost youth. Those in the town who would have the hippies and travellers go somewhere else should remember that they are part of its unique character and an endless fascination to tourists. Remove them with a swathe of intolerance and you rip the heart out of Glastonbury, for tolerance of alternative lifestyles is what makes Glastonbury special. Glastonbury without the alternative community would be another dull market town with a few sorry ruins to show the tourist spillover from Clarks Village. Someone has to keep the memory alive, reminding all who visit that the Isle of Avalon is the fulcrum of the Grail Quest.

Before you leave the Tor look South and find the needle shape of the Hood Monument, framed by the cut through the woods so that the Tor and the monument are intervisible. This was the start of our Quest, the point from which Perceval first set out for Arthur's court in search of the illusory glister of knighthood. Enjoy too, the long profile of Wearyall Hill, looking for all the world like a vast, beached whale, where we first encountered the mysterious Grail Castle — which may materialise at any moment and in any place to the knight who is ready to behold its mysteries.

Clustered around us is the sprawl of modern Glastonbury, extending inexorably toward the sea moor. Planners scratch their heads in the search for building space. Even the sea moor isn't safe from development. Anyone who jumps up and down on the peat and feels the ground wobble like a jelly beneath their feet will understand the problems of building on wetland. But the great Mammon has designed concrete rafts and piles driven thirty or forty feet through the soft peat to build even here. The Mother bides her time. She knows that a handful of pumps and a scatter of ditches will not alter her way of doing things. One day she will reclaim what we have taken.

It is time to return. *Descend the hill toward the town until you reach the path down to Wellhouse Lane.* Here the Red and White Springs once flowed down a pretty valley from the caves above, before nineteenth century vandalism built the reservoir. Perhaps one day they will demolish the reservoir and the pump house above (now a private dwelling) and restore the magic that lies buried in the earth.

The vault beneath the reservoir is now a café and its dark, humid, candle-lit space with attendant streams of water and iconography of alternative culture create a heady environment. Past Wellhouse Lane, along Chilkwell Street, we come to Chalice Well Gardens. This space is run by a Trust, founded by Wellesley Tudor Pole, a leading figure in the growth of modern interest in the mysteries of Avalon. *If you turn right at the road junction, to walk past the Abbey House, now a retreat centre for the diocese of Bath and Wells, you will come back to the start of your walk.*

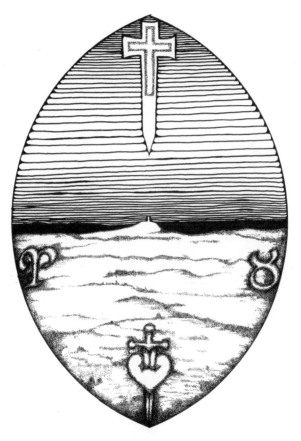

What was expected of the Quest Knight when he faced the Fisher King once more is that he will ask the question that he neglected to ask so long ago when he wore the crown of innocence:

"What ails you?"

Perceval could not ask the question the first time precisely because he was innocent. He did not know who he was and had assumed the masks of others. He had stolen the armour of a man he had killed for no just reason — a close relative at that. He was responsible for the death of his mother and neglected, for years after her death, even to ask of her. He came across a man in dreadful suffering and out of naïve politeness said nothing to console him. Perceval sinned and did not know it. He had no real understanding of the nature of evil.

His awareness, like ours, came with the Fall. It fell like a pall on the shoulders of humanity when we ate of the fruit of the Tree of Knowledge of Good and Evil. When Perceval confronts the Fisher King once more and asks the Question he has attained wisdom and self-knowledge. Like Christ, he must take on his shoulders the psychic pain of his generation. In so doing he transcends himself and is taken up — to Sarras, to Paradise, call it what you will — having become, like the Grail itself, too good for this world.

In simpler terms, he has removed the masks he had made for himself and found the Grail within. The entire universe that whirls about our heads is a mirror of our soul. There and there alone we must search for our own Sarras. We must look to ourselves to find Eden.

Now we have come down from the mountain, we may reflect upon our experience. Once more, we must take up the burdens of the daily round. Has nothing changed? In removing the Mask of Pretence, and accepting, as Camus would have us, the essential absurdity of our lives, we may have found the Grail — for today, perhaps. As for tomorrow — well, tomorrow is another day:

"I leave Sisyphus at the foot of the mountain! One always finds one's burden again. But Sisyphus teaches the higher fidelity that negates the gods and raises rocks. He, too, concludes that all is well. This universe henceforth without a master seems to him neither sterile nor futile. Each atom of that stone, each mineral flake of that night-filled mountain, in itself forms a world. The struggle itself towards the heights is enough to fill a man's heart. One must imagine Sisyphus happy." [17]

The Quest is an endless struggle, pushing our own burden of life up the Spiral Hill, in the hope that, when we reach the top, all will be well. Too often, like Sisyphus, we find ourselves at the bottom again. The Quest — the endless struggle to be worthy of the Grail is all, and it is the essence of our humanity.

1. see Philip Rahtz, Glastonbury, (English Heritage/ B.T. Batsford, 1993) P.59

2. John Matthews, Temples of the Grail, essay published in At the Table of the Grail Editor John Matthews, (Routledge & Kegan Paul, 1984) P84

3. Wolfram von Eschenbach, Parzival, written circa 1210, trans A.T. Hatto.(Penguin Books, 1986) P.369

4. ibid., 4. P.371

5. Herne, History and Antiquities of Glastonbury, 1772, re-published in A Glastonbury Reader, compiled by John Matthews, (Aquarian/Thorsons 1991) P27

6. Wolfram von Eschenbach, P.401

7. ibid., P.403

8. ibid., P.405

9. see Julius Evola, The Mystery of the Grail, trans. Guido Stucco, (first pub. 1934. This ed., Inner Traditions International, Rochester, Vermont 1997) P.48

10.Wolfram von Eschenbach, P.388

11. ibid., P392

12. ibid., P.393

13. Emma Jung & Marie-Louise von Franz, The Grail Legend, trans. Andrea Dykes, (Sigo Press, Boston 1986) P.344

14. Wolfram von Eschenbach, P.394

15. The Upanishads, trans. Juan Mascaro, (Harmondsworth, Penguin Books, 1965) 8:1

16. Wolfram von Eschenbach, P.402

17. Albert Camus. The Myth of Sisyphus, trans. Justin O'Brien, first published 1955. (Penguin Twentieth-Century Classics, 1975) P.111

Glastonbury Abbey

A Meditation on Arthur and the
Fellowship of the Table Round

OW put me into the barge, said the king. And so he did softly; and there received him three queens with great mourning; and so they set them down, and in one of their laps King Arthur laid his head. And then that queen said: Ah, dear brother, why have ye tarried so long from me? Alas, this wound on your head hath caught over-much cold. And so they rowed from the land, and Sir Bedivere beheld all these ladies go from him. Then Sir Bedivere cried: Ah my lord Arthur, what shall become of me, now ye go from me and leave me here alone among mine enemies? Comfort thyself, said the king, and do as well as thou mayst, for in me is no trust for to trust in; for I will into the vale of Avilion, to heal me of my grievous wound: and if thou hear never more of me, pray for my soul." [1]

The now indissoluble link between Arthur and Glastonbury was already three hundred years old when Sir Thomas Malory wrote these words. In 1184 a terrible fire had swept away the Saxon and Norman monastery. In the building work that followed, a coffin made out of a hollowed oak trunk had been discovered in the old cemetery to the south of what is now the Lady Chapel. The monks claimed they had found the remains of Arthur and his queen, Guinevere. At Easter 1278, the bones were translated in the presence of Edward I and Queen Eleanor to a fine black marble tomb before the high altar in the magnificent new abbey. By this time, the remains of King Arthur and Queen Guinevere had become the monastery's most significant relics. But Arthur was not Glastonbury's earliest claim to fame. Rather, it was the association with Joseph of Arimathea, who legend says built the first Church in Christendom where the Lady Chapel now stands. The same fire that destroyed the abbey swept away the Old Church — a structure of wattle and thatch, which was venerated as that most ancient church.

Some legends went further, stating that Joseph brought the Sangreal to Glastonbury — the sacred relics of the passion of Jesus — the Cup of the Last Supper and the Blood and Sweat of the Crucified.

Modern excavation has revealed evidence of a Celtic Christian community and there is little doubt that the enduring myth of the antiquity of the Church at Glastonbury is rooted in the presence of a Christian community since time beyond remembering. From its simple beginnings of wattle and daub huts the church grew into the wealthiest and most powerful monastic community in the country and boasted some of Christendom's most magnificent architecture. Anyone visiting Wells Cathedral will get some indication of what is lost, for a more magnificent building than this was torn down in the years following the Dissolution.

At the turn of the century and even as late as the 1920s both popular and scholarly opinion argued the presence of Joseph of Arimathea at Glastonbury as an historical fact, along with the coming of Arthur and the abbacy of St. Patrick. Scholarly opinion has moved on, and Glastonbury's foremost modern archaeologist, Philip Rahtz, regards the legends as something of a hindrance to progress toward a real understanding of the town's history. In discussing prevailing attitudes to the Glastonbury myths, he describes himself as subscribing to the following viewpoint:

> "They are not true, but are wholly the product of medieval and later invention, for pecuniary, political or prestige motives; their continued exposition as fact degrades real scholarship and historical truth, which should be exciting enough without the embroidery of myth elevated to fact." [2]

But Glastonbury *is* its myths and the Glastonbury that is famed around the world lives best in the heart and the imagination. The rather dowdy modern town, with its ever-growing rash of poorly planned development, would barely merit a single book if it were not for the overwhelming presence of that other Glastonbury. The last century has seen literally hundreds of books written about Glastonbury, as each generation of pilgrims attempt to make sense of its special magic.

I agree with Rahtz, in so far as the confusion of myth for history damages the integrity of both. Myth and History gain nothing from bending a tissue of archaeology to give us the 'history' behind the myth. The search for the 'historical' Arthur reduced Britain's most potent archetype to a grubby local warlord leading a war band of a hundred or so hearth companions dressed in the rusting cast-offs of Roman legionaries.

Arthur, the Round Table and the Quest for the Holy Grail are so much more than this. They are the supreme expression of the medieval spirit. They symbolise the passions and aspirations that underpinned an entire society. The tortured spirits of the Quest Knights express the yearnings, hopes, and aspirations of the chivalrous age. Chretien de Troyes and Wolfram von Eschenbach enable us to feel the pounding heart of the knight waiting beneath the gaze of his ladylove for his turn at the joust, and the passion of the Templar fighting the infidel beneath the walls of old Jerusalem.

Those who ponder the sorry ruins of Glastonbury Abbey and reflect upon its former glory should consider that it was the myth of a God incarnate that raised these stones in the first place, and raised every cathedral in medieval Europe. All that Man has achieved existed first as myths and dreams.

Modernity has witnessed the death of Myth. Demythologising has emptied the heavens of gods and the world of dreams. The product logo has replaced the eternal symbols, which once gave us our identity. We are no longer individuals, but consumers.

And it was the first cold wind of modernity that led to the abandonment of Glastonbury's myths and a new zeitgeist that tore down the edifice of the past. What the visitor sees today, when they visit the abbey, are not the predations of time but over three hundred years of looting. The search for Paradise has been abandoned and the symbols of that Quest destroyed.

Truth is a product of the heart and the imagination. It is the heart and the imagination that breathes life into the fragment of pottery and the rusting sword. It is the heart and the imagination that creates the church and the feasting hall out of the shadows in the grass. Ask not if Arthur and the Grail existed or if Joseph of Arimathea truly rested on Wearyall Hill and bore the Grail to Avalon. There is no surer truth. The myth of Arthur and the Holy Grail is Glastonbury and will endure when the salt sea has swept modern Glastonbury away.

Truth is a matter of faith. Without faith, these gaunt ruins could not speak to us. The voyage, across undefined stretches of water and through barren wastelands and endless forests in search of the Holy Grail is nothing without faith. Likewise, our own journeying through the vale of life is nothing without faith.

In the Queste del Saint Graal, the ship that carried Perceval, Galahad and Bors to Sarras and the fulfillment of the Quest bore this legend:

"GIVE EAR, O MAN WHO WOULDST SET FOOT IN ME: WHOSOEVER THOU ART, TAKE HEED THAT THOU BE FULL OF FAITH, FOR I AM FAITH ITSELF. THEREFORE LOOK TO IT, ERE THOU ENTEREST HERE, THAT THOU BE WITHOUT SPOT, FOR I AM NOUGHT BUT FAITH AND TRUE BELIEF, AND AS SOON AS THOU DOST LAPSE FROM FAITH, MYSELF SHALL CAST THEE DOWN IN SUCH A WAY THAT THOU SHALT FIND IN ME NOR HELP NOR FOOTING, BUT I SHALL FAIL THEE WHOLLY," [3]

Reflections in the Grounds of Glastonbury Abbey

"...From our old books I know
That Joseph came of old to Glastonbury,
And there the heathen Prince, Arviragus,
Gave him an isle of marsh whereon to build;
And there he built with wattles from the marsh
A little lonely church in days of yore." [4]

At the West End of the abbey, which is the first part of the ruins we encounter as we leave the visitor centre, stands the Lady Chapel. This beautiful late romanesque chapel is the best-preserved part of the abbey. Stripped of most of its ornament and roofless, its four walls still stand, reflecting a simplicity of style and proportion that was lost by the time the newly built abbey of the thirteenth century had risen to the skies.

Perhaps local superstition had something to do with its preservation. Long before the grandeur of the medieval abbey, a simple wattle church, known as the Old Church, stood on this spot, surrounded by a cluster of monastic cells. This is the church that Arthur would have known. Early medieval authors, including the anonymous eleventh century biographer of St. Dunstan, perpetuate the legend that the first church at Glastonbury was not the work of men, but had a heavenly builder. Indeed, it is described by Marson as the first church to be built, not only in England, but the world:

"St. Joseph and his friends built of mud and wattle the first Christian Church, not only in Britain but in the world. He built it of mud and wattle, thatched with reed in the style of the land, and made it 60 feet long, by 25 wide. There, in the eastern fashion, the disciples lived in their separate huts." [5]

Walking into the Lady Chapel, we find ourselves on a modern iron balcony that overlooks the crypt. Known as St. Joseph's Chapel, the crypt is named after Joseph of Arimathea, the bringer of the Grail to Avalon.

Frederick Bligh Bond believed that the Old Church known to medieval historians, was built directly over the site of an older circular church and twelve monastic cells built around it. The Old Church and what remnant there might have been of the earlier circular structure disappeared in the great fire of AD 1184.

The excavation of the ground beneath the Lady Chapel to create St. Joseph's Chapel would have destroyed what remained of the foundations of the Old Church and its predecessor. We may imagine that the Lady Chapel and its crypt still enshrines the ghost of the Old Church of wattle, hovering in the hollow space and sensed by the coldness that lingers here, even on a summer day.

Bligh Bond believed that he had found evidence for the foundations for two of the tiny cells that formed the perfect circle of twelve cells around the first of Christian churches. Thus, the sacred space that one gazes into from the crypt beneath the Lady Chapel was once the very hub of faith, the manifestation of the Round Table and the space in which the Companions of that Fellowship venerated the Sangreal. [6]

He believed that the twelve cells symbolise the Zodiac and connected the Round Table with the rotunda of the sky and our heavenly destiny.

Legend says that Joseph of Arimathea died and was buried here. Despite the monastery's huge collection of relics and the claim to have unearthed the bones of Arthur and his queen, the monks of Glastonbury never claimed to have found the bones of Joseph of Arimathea. In the years following the Dissolution, William Good, a former acolyte of the monastery, testified that:

"The monks never knew for certain the place of this saint's burial or pointed it out. They said the body was hidden most carefully, either there or on a hill near Montacute called Hamden Hill, and that when his body should be found, the whole world should wend their way thither on account of the number and wondrous nature of the miracles worked there." [7]

An ancient sarcophagus rescued from the abbey and now in the church of St. John's on the High Street, is claimed by some to have once marked his burial place. Some believe that wherever he lies, he guards the Sangreal still:

"With him he carried two silver cruets with the precious Blood and Water washed from our Saviour's wounds, which cruets were buried with him in the sacred cemetery and are some day to be discovered." [8]

"We, as Christians, believe that Joseph took down from the Cross the body of the Master, Jesus. It is no stretch of the imagination

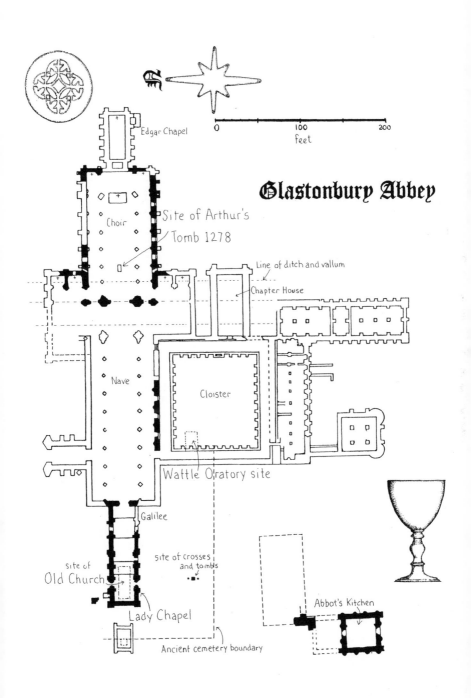

Edgar Chapel

Glastonbury Abbey

Choir

Site of Arthur's Tomb 1278

Line of ditch and vallum

Chapter House

Nave

Cloister

Wattle Oratory site

Galilee

site of crosses and tombs

site of Old Church

Lady Chapel

Ancient cemetery boundary

Abbot's Kitchen

to realize that he would have taken the utmost pains to secure for all time that most precious relic of all, a phial of His Blood. And this he brought to Glaston, where, by tradition, it lies buried beneath the soil — not to reappear until the time is ripe for its revelation." [9]

It is also claimed that Joseph of Arimathea brought with him the Cup of the Last Supper. Carved from a ruby that once adorned the crown of Lucifer, the Stone had been struck from his armour by St. Michael and fell to earth. Here sea creatures carved it into a cup, which no man knew of, until King Solomon discovered it by divination. He used demons to bring it to him from the seabed. In time, it was given to the Saviour, who used it at the Last Supper. This cup was brought by Joseph to Glastonbury and after his death was kept in a treasury on Chalice Hill. Now it is in Sarras, the Spiritual City, and beyond the eyes of men, to return when we are worthy once more for it to dwell amongst us.

But much more is claimed of this little wattle church than the presence of Joseph of Arimathea. Legend says that Jesus and the Blessed Virgin accompanied Joseph to Glastonbury when Jesus was a boy. By the power of God, a church was built, so that the Christ Child might honour His Virgin Mother. Thus, what might be called the Sangreal came in the form of the Christ child Himself. In later years people testified to experiencing their presence. Lionel Smithett Lewis, one time Vicar of Glastonbury and author of a book on Glastonbury's sacred history, talks of his own reverence for the spot where Jesus and His Mother may well have stood:

> "On the South side of St. Mary's Chapel, the Norman successor of the old wattle church, there appears in the wall a little old stone with two names "Jesus Maria"in large archaic letters... Why suddenly in that wall do those names appear? The monks evidently attached a great veneration to the stone. Did the feet of these holy beings ever tread this spot? I instinctively take off my hat when I approach it. It is a hallowed spot... The very possibility sanctifies beyond all words. One hopes it is true. And those who seek may find. It makes our Lord seem very near." [10]

For Frederick Bligh Bond, the myth of Joseph of Arimathea and his companions overshadows that of Arthur. The Fellowship of twelve knights who sat with Arthur at the Round Table was a symbolic manifestation of the fellowship of the twelve followers of Joseph of Arimathea. The legend of Arthur and the Round Table was ultimately the legend of how Christianity came to these shores:

"In the great tapestry of the Glastonbury tradition the story of Arthur, the British prince and his Twelve Knights is inevitably coupled with that of Joseph of Arimathea and his Company of Twelve. The Round Table of Arthur clearly reflects the form of Joseph's first settlement, just as the Twelve Knights are the symbolic counterparts of his company of fellow-missioners." [11]

Bligh Bond claimed to have unearthed evidence for the existence of the circular church and the twelve cells of Joseph of Arimathea's companions. Shortly thereafter, he received instructions from the church authorities to cease digging. The publication of his book, 'The Gate of Remembrance', in which he claimed to have located two important chapels through communicating with a dead monk and by automatic writing led to his dismissal by the church authorities. The various excavation trenches around the Lady Chapel were filled in and his speculations ignored. [12]

Bligh Bond's inspiration for linking the fellowship of the twelve knights of the Round Table with the twelve companions of Joseph, probably came from the 'Quest del Saint Graal'. Here the story is told of how Perceval visited a recluse and was to discover the history of that fellowship that was the noblest in the world. The recluse lived in a secluded house with a chapel close by, where she spent most of her hours.

In the crypt of St. Joseph, kneeling before the altar, see the veiled form of the recluse. We may not speak to her directly for she is confined to the chapel until the morrow. Her retainers told Perceval that he would be able to speak to her after holy mass the following day.

Following morning mass he presented himself to the noble woman, saying:

"Madam, for the love of God give me some tidings of the knight who passed here today, and with whom, as you told him, you are well acquainted."

She replied:

"Ah! Perceval, what are you saying? Would you measure yourself with him? Are you anxious to die like your brothers, who perished victims of their own arrogance? Are you aware of what you would be losing by joining battle with this knight? Let me tell you then. It is true that the great Quest of the Holy Grail is begun, among whose companions you, I believe, are numbered, and it will shortly be brought to its close, so it please God. And at its term a far higher honour than you thought to find awaits you, if you will but refrain from breaking lances with that knight."

Perceval asked once more about the knight he sought and by what right he had made his demands at Arthur's Court. She replied:

"You are well aware that since the advent of Christ Jesus the world has seen three great fellowships. The first was the table of Jesus Christ, where the apostles broke bread on many occasions. That was the table where the bread of heaven sustained both souls and bodies, while they that sat round it were one in heart and soul, as King David prophesied when he wrote in his book the wonderful words: "Behold how good and how pleasant it is for brethren to dwell together in unity." Peace and long-suffering and concord reigned among the brethren seated at that table, and all good works could be seen in them; and that table was established by the lamb without spot who was sacrificed for our redemption."

She explained to Perceval that the second fellowship was established shortly after the crucifixion of Jesus, when Joseph of Arimathea and his followers established the Table of the Holy Grail when they first came to this land:

"This table was succeeded by the Round Table, devised by Merlin to embody a very subtle meaning. For in its name it mirrors the roundness of the earth, the concentric spheres of the planets and of the elements of the firmament; and in these heavenly spheres we see the stars and many things besides; whence it follows that the Round Table is a true epitome of the universe.... When Merlin had established the Round Table, he announced that the secrets of the Holy Grail, which in his time was covert and withdrawn, would be revealed by knights of that same fellowship."

Merlin went on to prophesy the outcome of the Quest for the Grail:

"There will be three shall triumph in this undertaking: two will be virgins, and the other chaste. And one of the three shall surpass his father in strength as the lion surpasses the leopard in strength and hardihood. He shall be held as master and shepherd over all his fellows; and the companions of the Round Table will consume their days in bootless pursuit of the Holy Grail until such time as Our Lord shall send him among them so suddenly as to confound them all."

Those who heard the prophecy asked Merlin how the worthy knight might be known. Merlin said that he would fashion a new Siege Perilous, which would bring destruction to all who sat in it, except the one who was worthy:

"Good nephew,"continued the lady, "I have explained to you how the Round Table came to be established, and the Seat of Danger too, where many a knight has perished who was unfit to sit there." [13]

Thus, the Table of the Last Supper, the Table at which the Fellowship of Joseph of Arimathea broke bread together, and the Fellowship of the Round Table are all part of the one tradition. All are tables at which the Holy Grail manifested itself, and nourished those who were worthy enough to be called to that Supper.

On the south side of the Lady Chapel is the site of the ancient cemetery of the monastic community. The use of this ground as a burial place predates both the medieval and Saxon monastery. St. Dunstan, who was abbot between 940 and 956, had the holy earth surrounded by a wall and the ground level raised to protect the sacred remains. This was why more than thirteen feet of earth covered the oak coffin in which Arthur's bones were found. James Carley speaks poetically of the importance of the cemetery to the monastic community:

"The sanctity of Glastonbury's cemetery would provide a constant solace to the monks. The burials represented an unbroked tradition of worship; each new grave increased the total effect. Unlike a modern cemetery, where our thoughts are directed towards death and disintegration, this site struck awe and a sense of God's nearness into the heart of the observer; its numinosity was so powerful that a touch of the sacred soil acted in itself as a kind of intercession at the seat of God." [14]

Tradition states that this was regarded by many as the most holy ground of all, sanctified by the relics of those who had prayed to God, each in his time, since the earliest days of Christendom. John of Glastonbury records how a Crusader, one Rainald of Marksbury, was able to pay his ransom from the sultan who had captured him with a gloveful of earth from this cemetery, so famous was its power to sanctify. Anyone who was at rest within its sacred precincts was surely in Paradise for the earth itself would reject the bones of the unworthy.

Within the boundaries of this ancient cemetery modern archaeologists have found post-holes of at least four oratories of a wattle type, similar to those discovered at other Celtic monasteries, adding to the evidence of the age and sanctity of this spot.

The simple metal plaque by the path has this to say:

"Site of the ancient graveyard where in 1191 the monks dug to find the tomb of Arthur and Guinevere."

The words are inadequate. The holy men who lived and died here, be they saints or sinners, kings or paupers, were laid to rest in this holy ground. Now it is a lawn, and in the absence of more fitting memorials we may stroll across it as we might any other patch of grass. But pause awhile. Kneel and touch this sacred earth. If Arthur lies in Avalon, then it is here that the earth is sanctified with his blood. The holy men of old, who built that first church of wattle and thatch, sleep beneath your feet. If Joseph came to Avalon then he lies here too and perhaps — who knows? — the blood of Christ Himself. Do what they would have wanted of you. Speak to them. Pray for the souls of those who do not already walk in the gardens of Paradise. Ask those who already see God to pray for you.

Here, between the foundations of two stone pyramids — just as the medieval texts describe — the archaeologist, Raleigh Radford, found the evidence that a hole had been dug and filled in shortly thereafter. He found evidence of two or three slab-lined graves from the earliest days of the monastic community, indicating that the monks had indeed disturbed a very ancient grave. The grave of Arthur? Well, I like to think not because I do not like to think of Arthur as dead. For those who seek the Arthur of history, I have this to say: if Arthur has a grave, then the cemetery at Glastonbury is where he lies. For me, Arthur sleeps and has no grave.

If we walk along the south side of the Lady Chapel and down a simple flight of steps, we may enter the Galilee. This beautiful space was built to link the Lady Chapel with the nave of the abbey, thus creating the longest church in the land other that the old St. Paul's in London. As we gaze up the steps that once led to the west end of this earthly paradise, we may try to reconstruct that grandeur in our imagination. Two rows of mighty pillars support the magnificent gothic arches of the bays, the clerestories above support the stone vaulting that seems to grow organically from the foliated capitals, like the overarching canopy of a forest. The sun streams through the myriad panels of stained glass that illumine the eternal truths in images and symbols that have shaped a civilization. Every carved corbel and capital speaks to us, every statue, and painted image. The senses are overwhelmed by the flickering of a thousand candles, the clouds of precious incense rising to the throne of God and the pure, unaccompanied voices of the monks chanting in the low, even rhythms of St. Gregory.

A great and colourful throng fills the church. Surrounded by a hundred knights and retainers, King Edward, Queen Eleanor, the Archbishop of Canterbury and Abbot John of Taunton, preside over the most magnificent ceremonial the abbey has seen. The focus is the gilded chests containing the bones of King Arthur and his Queen. The gilded chests bear the portraits of Arthur and Queen Guinevere. The queen's portrait showed her fully crowned. Arthur's portrait showed him wearing a battle-damaged crown and the bloody marks of the wounds that killed him. [15]

In his baggage, Edward carries another crown — the crown of Arthur — taken from Llywelyn, Prince of Wales as a trophy of his conquest of the Celtic people. It seems to him that this ceremony seals the fate of the Celtic kingdoms of Wales and Scotland. The king of the Britons is dead and his bones lie in the earth. Arthur is no more and Edward is now their king.

We smile, being wise. Like the head of Bran gazing from London's Tower toward the cold sea, we know that Arthur watches and waits his time. This elaborate fiction does not fool the ghosts who had ridden from Camelot to curse the upstart king.

How mightily the choir sings, as the bones are laid within the black marble tomb that has been built before the high altar, with its four lions and effigy of Arthur! Such splendour, such ceremony will not be seen again in our lifetimes!

Edward and his queen are dead, the black marble tomb was carted off long ago, and the great, vaulted space of Glastonbury Abbey has given way to the dome of the sky. Such are the vanities of this world. Nourished from that ruby cup that once knew the blood of Jesus, Arthur sleeps in that middle space between the earth and the sky. He, whose fame and exploits eclipsed the deeds of all monarchs before and since will come again.

Just after the transept, at the entrance to what was once the choir, the shrine of King Arthur is marked today by a simple concrete kerb and a painted metal plaque. The text reads:

> "Site of King Arthur's Tomb. In the year 1191 the bodies of King Arthur and his Queen were said to have been found on the south side of the Lady Chapel. On 19th April 1278 their remains were removed in the presence of King Edward I and Queen Eleanor to a black marble tomb on this site. The tomb survived until the dissolution of the abbey in 1539."

In the stillness of a summer afternoon as you gaze at this nondescript metal plaque remember that Arthur is not here and never was.

He is "Rex Quondam, Rex Futurus" — The Once and Future King

Scholarly opinion places the writing of 'Perlesvaus', which sets the Grail Legend in the Glastonbury landscape, to about 1200. Written in Old French prose for a Flemish lord, it illustrates the fact that our own Quest is rooted in an eight hundred-year-old tradition. When the debunkers and their books have long rotted away, the tale of Perceval and the Quest for the Grail will stand, for it is written in men's hearts for all to read who are prepared to look there.

"Here ends the holy story of the Grail. Josephus, who recorded it, gives the blessing of Our Lord to all who hear it and honour it. The Latin text from which this story was set down in the vernacular was taken from the Isle of Avalon, from a holy religious house which stands at the edge of the Lands of Adventure; there lie King Arthur and the queen, by the testimony of the worthy religious men who dwell there, and who have the whole story, true from the beginning to the end." [16]

1. Sir Thomas Malory Le Morte D'Arthur, (first pub. 1485, this edition Wordsworth Editions Limited, 1996)

2. Philip Rahtz, Glastonbury, (Batsford/ English Heritage 1993) P42

3. Quest del Saint Graal, Author unknown, trans. Pauline Matarasso, (Penguin Classic) P212

4. Alfred Lord Tennyson, The Holy Grail, from Idylls of the King, (Henry King & Co., 1875) P259

5. L. Marson, Glastonbury: The Historic Guide to the English Jerusalem, (George Gregory, Bath, 1909) P7)

6. Frederick Bligh Bond, The Mystery of Glastonbury, 1930, reprinted in A Glastonbury Reader, edit. John Matthews (Aquarian/ Thorsons, 1991) P199ff

7. quoted by James P. Carley, Glastonbury Abbey, (Gothic Image Publications, 1996) P123

8. L.Marson, P6

9.Bligh Bond, P209

10. Lionel Smithett Lewis, St. Joseph of Arimathea at Glastonbury, —. first pub. in 1922. This edition 1988, (James Clarke & Co Ltd, Cambridge) P.59

11. Frederick Bligh Bond, P203

12. see Frederick Bligh Bond, The Gate of Remembrance, (Basil Blackwell, Oxford, 1918)

13. Queste del Saint Graal, P95ff

14. James P. Carley, P145

15. The account of the translation of the bones of Arthur to the new tomb was enclosed within the tomb at the time of Edward's visit and is now preserved in the Bodleian Library, Oxford. See James P. Carley, P37

16. Anonymous author of Perlesvaus, trans. Nigel Bryant, (D S Brewer, Cambridge, 1978. This edition 1996) P265